ORIGO
STEPPING STONES
2.0
COMPREHENSIVE MATHEMATICS

AUTHORS

James Burnett
Calvin Irons
Peter Stowasser
Allan Turton

PROGRAM CONSULTANTS

Diana Lambdin
Frank Lester, Jr.
Kit Norris

CONTRIBUTING WRITERS

Donna Arnott   Beth Lewis
Debi DePaul   Melanie Theed
Jaye Kelly

STUDENT BOOK A

ORIGO
EDUCATION

INTRODUCTION

ORIGO STEPPING STONES 2.0 STUDENT JOURNAL

ORIGO Stepping Stones 2.0 is a comprehensive program that brings conceptual understanding of mathematics to the forefront of teaching and learning. The Student Journal consists of two parts: Book A (Modules 1–6) and Book B (Modules 7–12). Each book contains lessons, practice pages, and Developing the practices, plus a complete Contents and Student Glossary.

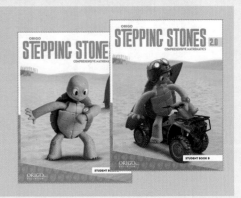

LESSON PAGES

There are two pages for each of the 12 lessons in every module. This sample shows the key components.

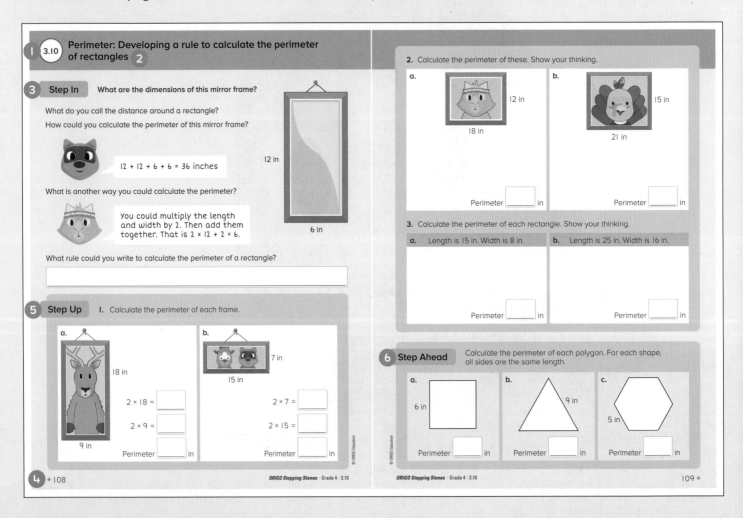

1. Module number and lesson number.

2. The lesson title tells the content of the lesson. It has two parts: the stem (or big idea), and the leaf (which gives more details).

3. Step In is designed to generate classroom discourse. Open questions are posed to make students think about different methods or answers.

4. For Grade 4, Book A shows a teal diamond beside each page number. Book B shows a purple diamond.

5. Step Up provides appropriate written work for the student.

6. Step Ahead puts a twist on each lesson to develop higher-order thinking skills.

INTRODUCTION

PRACTICE PAGES

Lessons 2, 4, 6, 8, 10, and 12 each provide two pages for maintaining concepts and skills. These samples show the key components.

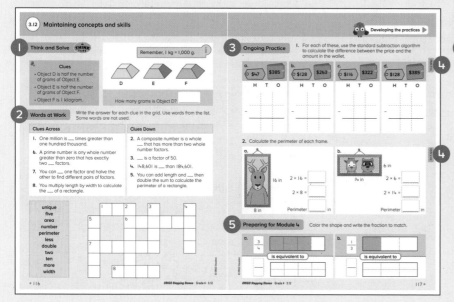 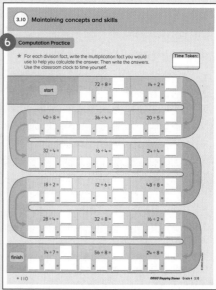

1. The *ORIGO Think Tanks* are a popular way for students to practice problem-solving. There are three Think Tank problems in each module.

2. The development of written language is essential. These activities aim to help students develop their academic vocabulary, and provide opportunities for students to write their thinking.

3. Ongoing Practice relates to content previously learned. Question 1 always revisits content from a previous module, and Question 2 revisits content from the current module.

4. This tab shows the original lesson.

5. Each right-hand page provides content that prepares students for the next module.

6. Regular written practice of mental strategies is essential. There are three computation practice pages that focus on specific strategies in each module.

7. Reinforce the Standards for Mathematical Practice by completing the Mathematical modeling task at the end of each module.

8. Develop skills to critique and reason by completing the Convince a friend task at the end of each module.

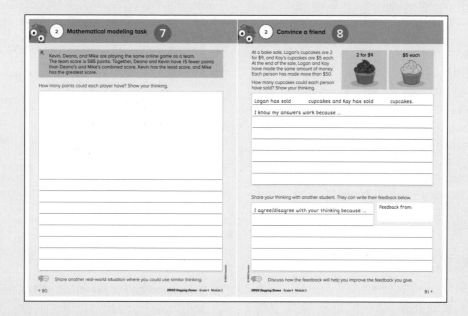

BOOK A CONTENTS

ORIGO Stepping Stones • Grade 4

© ORIGO Education

BOOK B CONTENTS

Step In

What number is shown on each part of this mix-and-match card?

How does the number on the expander match the number shown on the abacus?

What numeral would you write to match the number?

_____ , _____

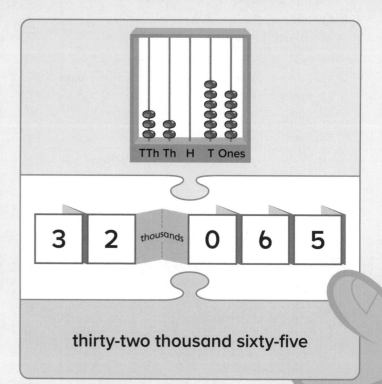

3 2 thousands 0 6 5

thirty-two thousand sixty-five

The comma separates the thousands place from the hundreds, tens, and ones. It helps you read the number.

How would you represent this number on a mix-and-match card?   70,912

Step Up

1. Draw beads on the abacus to represent the number.

a. 82,451

TTh Th H T Ones

b. 17,050

TTh Th H T Ones

c. 40,103

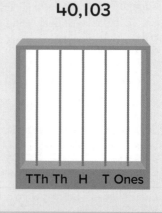

TTh Th H T Ones

ORIGO Stepping Stones · Grade 4 · 1.1

2. Complete the missing parts.

a.

_____

| 5 | 7 | thousands | 3 | 9 | 8 |

_____

b.

74,510

| | | thousands | | | |

_____

c.

_____

| | | thousands | | | |

eighteen thousand seven hundred ninety

d.

20,675

| | | thousands | | | |

_____

e.

_____

| | | thousands | | | |

thirty-six thousand forty-five

Step Ahead

Cross out any two beads. Then write the new number in words.

TTh Th H T Ones

_____

Step In What is the greatest five-digit number you can write?

_____ _____ , _____ _____ _____

What number would you say after this number?

What do you know about the number 100,000?

The human heart beats about 100,000 times each day!

Write 100,000 on this place-value chart.

What do you notice about each group of three places?

Thousands			Ones		
H	T	O	H	T	O

Look at the number on this abacus.

How do you know where to write the matching digits on this expander?

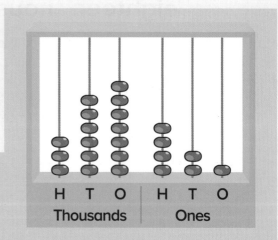

How do you say this number? What place values do you read together?

Step Up 1. Color ⬭ to show the answer that makes sense.

a.   A large tissue box full of uncooked rice holds about ...

   ◯ 1,000 grains   ◯ 10,000 grains   ◯ 100,000 grains

b.   The total length of 5 cars parked end-to-end is about ...

   ◯ 1,000 inches   ◯ 10,000 inches   ◯ 100,000 inches

2. Look at the abacus. Write the matching number on the expander.

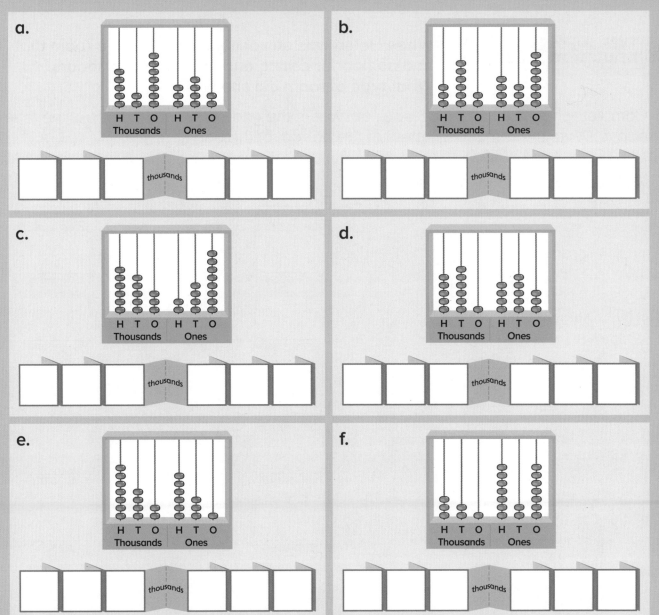

a.

b.

c.

d.

e.

f.

Step Ahead

Read the number on the expander. Then circle the abacus that shows a number that is 1,000 greater.

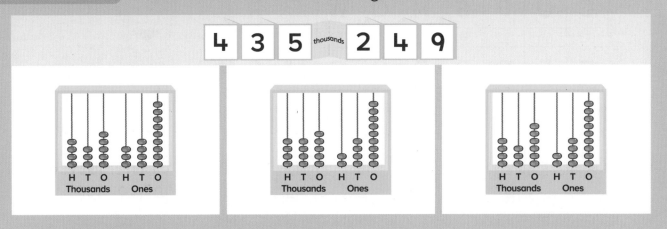

| 4 | 3 | 5 | *thousands* | 2 | 4 | 9 |

Computation Practice

When Helen was on vacation, she found a room that had no floor or ceiling and no windows or doors. What type of room did she find?

★ Complete the equations. Find each answer in the grid below and cross out the letter above. Write the remaining letters at the bottom of the page.

64 – 32 = ☐	12 + 13 = ☐	62 – 31 = ☐
42 + 43 = ☐	48 – 24 = ☐	21 + 22 = ☐
46 – 23 = ☐	41 + 42 = ☐	45 – 23 = ☐
22 + 22 = ☐	27 – 14 = ☐	14 + 15 = ☐
82 – 41 = ☐	22 + 23 = ☐	65 – 32 = ☐
32 + 31 = ☐	84 – 42 = ☐	24 – 24 = ☐

B	A	T	H	G	A	M	E	S
23	30	42	24	45	31	14	41	63
C	U	P	S	H	O	W	E	R
83	64	32	84	46	85	25	0	34
B	E	D	B	R	O	O	M	S
22	29	33	44	13	18	66	28	43

☐ ☐ ☐ ☐ ☐ ☐ ☐ ☐ ☐ ☐

Write the remaining letters in order from the ✳ to the bottom-right corner.

© ORIGO Education

Ongoing Practice

1. In each picture, one tens block has been regrouped for 10 ones blocks. Draw blocks in the small parts to show each share. Then complete the equation.

a.

$45 \div 3 = \boxed{}$

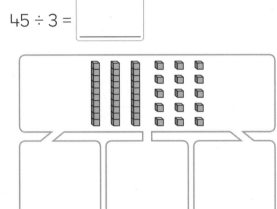

b.

$52 \div 4 = \boxed{}$

2. Draw extra beads on the abacus to match the number on the expander.

a.

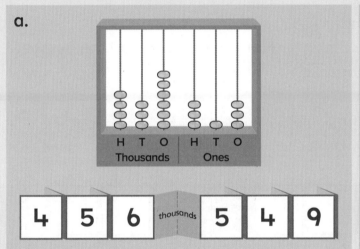

H	T	O	H	T	O
Thousands			Ones		

| 4 | 5 | 6 | *thousands* | 5 | 4 | 9 |

b.

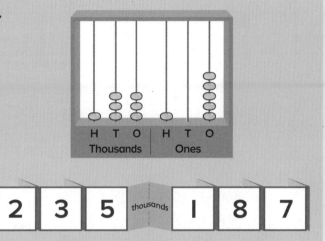

H	T	O	H	T	O
Thousands			Ones		

| 2 | 3 | 5 | *thousands* | 1 | 8 | 7 |

Preparing for Module 2

Estimate the total. Draw jumps on the number line to show how you formed your estimate.

a.   **45 + 29**

Estimate _____

b.   **92 + 35**

Estimate _____

© ORIGO Education

Step In

Imagine you used all three of these cards to show a single number.

Where would you write the digits for the number on the expander below? How do you know?

How would you read the number on the open expander?

The first three digits are all thousands, so you can put these places together and read the number of thousands.

Write the same number on this expander.

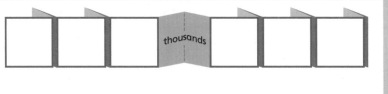

How would you read the number?

Step Up

I. Write the matching number on the expander.
    Then write the number in words.

a.

5 hundred thousands

2 hundreds

_____

_____

b.

6 hundred thousands

7 ten thousands

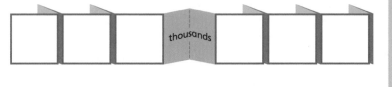

_____

_____

2. Calculate the values and write the matching number on the expander.
Then write the number in words.

a.

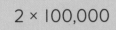

$2 \times 100{,}000$

5×100

_____

_____

b.

6×100

$3 \times 100{,}000$

4×10

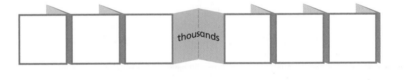

_____

_____

c.

7×1

$8 \times 100{,}000$

_____

_____

Step Ahead

Figure out the total number shown by each set of cards.
Write the numbers on the expanders below.

a.

| 5 0 0 | 4 0,0 0 0 |
| 6,0 0 0 | 3 0 0,0 0 0 |

b.

| 3 0 | 1 0 0,0 0 0 |
| 2,0 0 0 | 5 0,0 0 0 |

Number: Reading and writing six-digit numbers (with teens and zeros)

Step In

Write digits on the expander to match the number shown on the abacus.

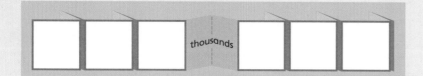

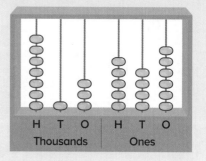

How could the expander help you figure out how to say the number name?

Write the number name.

Write the number on the expander to match this abacus.

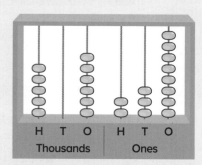

How would you say the number name?
How did the expander help you?

Step Up

1. Look at the abacus. Write the matching number on the expander. Then write the number name.

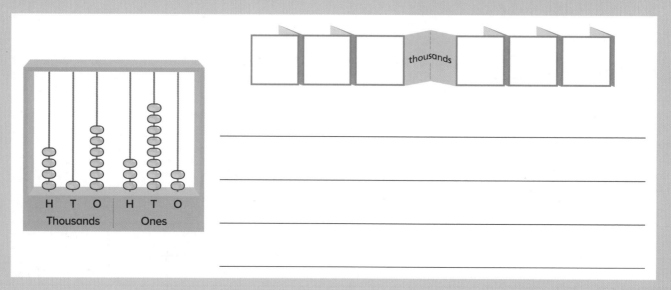

2. Write the matching numerals and number names. Draw beads on each blank abacus for the numeral shown.

a.

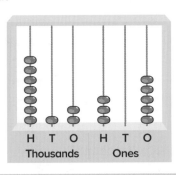

H T O   H T O
Thousands   Ones

_____

_____

_____

_____

b.

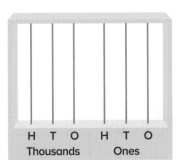

H T O   H T O
Thousands   Ones

584,300

_____

_____

_____

c.

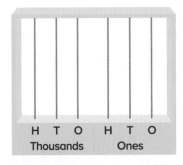

H T O   H T O
Thousands   Ones

_____

one hundred thousand

fifty-four

_____

Step Ahead

Write the value shown by the **3** in each number.
The first one has been done for you.

a. 463,759   **3,000**   **b.** 815,243 _____

c. 604,350 _____   **d.** 390,111 _____

e. 436,725 _____   **f.** 775,230 _____

Think and Solve Look at this arrow chart.

A | | B (×2, ×2, ×)

1. What number should appear in Box B, if

a. 6 is placed in Box A? ____

b. 30 is placed in Box A? ____

c. 35 is placed in Box A? ____

d. 12 is placed in Box A? ____

Working Space

2. What number should appear in the oval? ____

Words at Work   Write a numeral that has six digits. ____

Write about how you represent your number.

1. Read the division problem. Then complete each multiplication equation to help you form an estimate.

a.	86 ÷ 3

3 × 10 = _____

3 × 20 = _____

3 × 30 = _____

Estimate
_____

b.	54 ÷ 4

4 × 10 = _____

4 × 20 = _____

4 × 30 = _____

Estimate
_____

c.	94 ÷ 5

5 × 10 = _____

5 × 20 = _____

5 × 30 = _____

Estimate
_____

FROM 3.12.5

2. Complete the missing parts.

a.

480,716

			thousands			

_____

FROM 4.1.4

b.

_____

			thousands			

eight hundred twenty-nine thousand five hundred three

Use the standard algorithm to calculate the exact sum. Then estimate to check your answer.

a.	H	T	O
		6	5
+			7

b.	H	T	O
		7	6
+			9

c.	H	T	O
	1	3	9
+			3

Step In   Read the number on the expander.

How would you describe the value of each digit?

| 5 hundred thousands | 6 ten thousands | 0 thousands | 8 hundreds | 1 tens | 2 ones |

Write the missing numbers to show the number in expanded form.

(☐ × 100,000) + (☐ × 10,000) + (☐ × 100) + (☐ × 10) + (☐ × 1)

Which value has not been expanded?

> You do not have to expand the value of the zero in the thousands place.

Manuel expanded the same number in a different way.

(8 × 100) + (1 × 10) + (6 × 10,000) + (5 × 100,000) + (2 × 1)

What do you notice about his method?
Does it matter what order you expand each place value? Why not?

Step Up   1.   Write the missing numbers to show each six-digit number in expanded form.

a.   360,712

(_____ × 100,000) + (_____ × 10,000) + (_____ × 100) + (_____ × 10) + (_____ × 1)

b.   803,649

(_____ × 100,000) + (_____ × 1,000) + (_____ × 100) + (_____ × 10) + (_____ × 1)

c.   500,911

(_____ × 100,000) + (_____ × 100) + (_____ × 10) + (_____ × 1)

2. Write the number that has been expanded.

a.
$(2 \times 100{,}000) + (4 \times 1{,}000) + (9 \times 100) + (8 \times 10) + (1 \times 1)$

_____

b.
$(6 \times 100{,}000) + (8 \times 10{,}000) + (6 \times 1{,}000) + (4 \times 100) + (5 \times 1)$

_____

c.
$(4 \times 100{,}000) + (9 \times 1{,}000) + (5 \times 10)$

_____

3. Write each number in expanded form.

a.

625,386

_____

_____

b.

190,714

_____

_____

c.

530,500

_____

_____

d.

800,487

_____

_____

Step Ahead

These place values have been written out of order.
Figure out and write each number that has been expanded.

a.
$(7 \times 10) + (4 \times 100{,}000) + (1 \times 10{,}000) + (9 \times 100) + (3 \times 1)$

_____

b.
$(6 \times 100{,}000) + (8 \times 1) + (4 \times 10) + (6 \times 1{,}000)$

_____

Step In   Start at 7. Say each number on the card.

How do the numbers change?
Say the same pattern again starting at 3.

What number belongs at each mark on this number line?

How do you know?

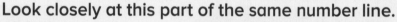

Look closely at this part of the same number line.

Draw marks on this part to show multiples of 1,000.

What numbers belong at these marks? Write two numbers.

Step Up   1. Draw a line to connect each number to its position
on the number line.

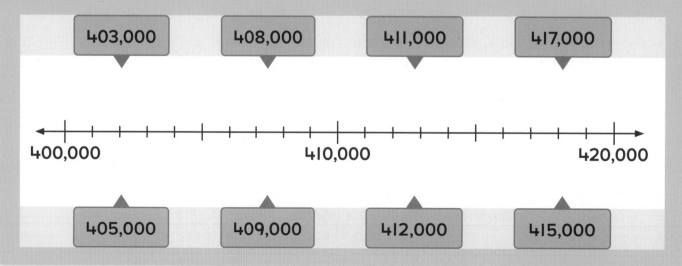

2. Look at each number line carefully. Write the number that is shown by each arrow.

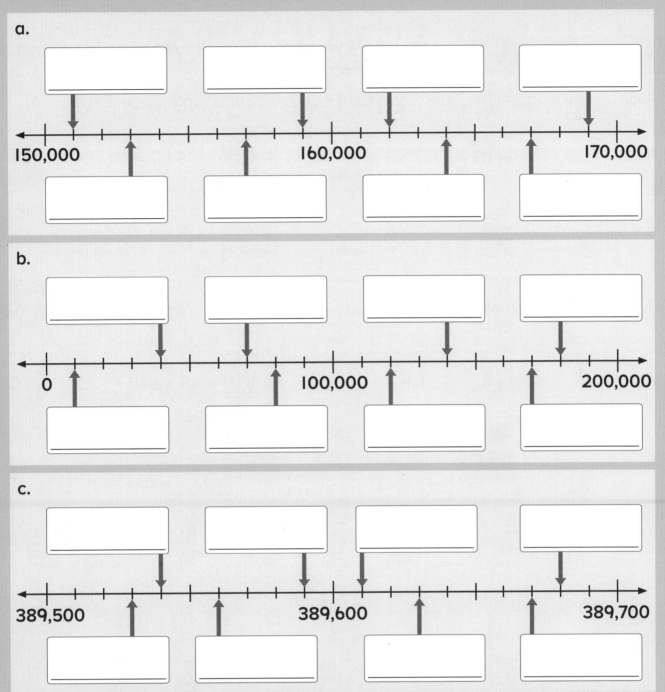

a.

b.

c.

Step Ahead

Odometers measure distance. These are odometer readings from vehicles that have just been serviced. If they are serviced every 50,000 miles, write the next service reading.

a.

3	0	0	0	0	0

						NEXT

b.

1	7	0	0	0	0

						NEXT

ORIGO Stepping Stones • Grade 4 • 1.6

21 ◆

© ORIGO Education

Computation Practice

I am where yesterday comes after today, and tomorrow is in between. What am I?

★ Complete the facts. Then write each letter above its matching product in the grid.

9 × 3 = ☐ **m**

7 × 9 = ☐ **a**

6 × 7 = ☐ **i**

8 × 6 = ☐ **i**

3 × 6 = ☐ **r**

5 × 9 = ☐ **i**

7 × 4 = ☐ **o**

7 × 7 = ☐ **a**

9 × 9 = ☐ **a**

8 × 3 = ☐ **t**

6 × 6 = ☐ **y**

9 × 6 = ☐ **c**

8 × 7 = ☐ **n**

7 × 5 = ☐ **d**

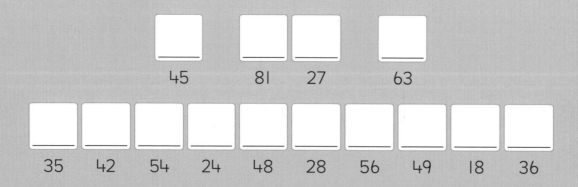

☐	☐	☐	☐
45	81	27	63

☐	☐	☐	☐	☐	☐	☐	☐	☐	☐
35	42	54	24	48	28	56	49	18	36

Complete these facts as fast as you can.

5 × 8 = ☐

7 × 3 = ☐

8 × 9 = ☐

4 × 6 = ☐

8 × 8 = ☐

3 × 5 = ☐

6 × 5 = ☐

8 × 4 = ☐

2 × 9 = ☐

1. Circle the objects that are prisms.

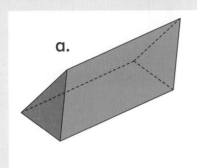
a.

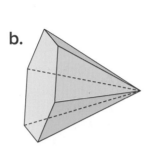
b.

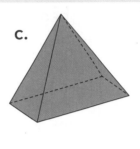
c.

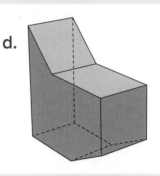
d.

FROM 3.12.8

2. Look at each number line carefully. Write the number that is shown by each arrow.

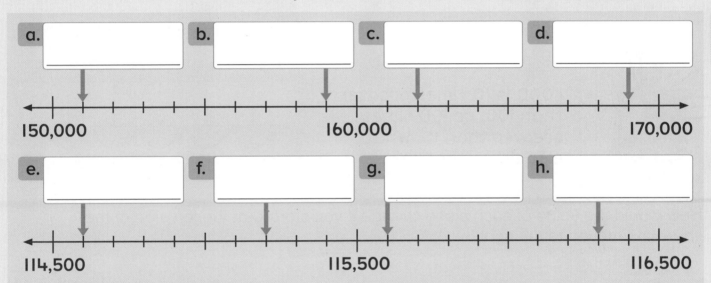

FROM 4.1.6

Preparing for Module 2

Use the standard algorithm to calculate the exact sum. Estimate to check your answer.

a.

	2	4	8
+		8	1

b.

	4	4	6
+		9	6

c.

	4	7	1
+		9	5

d.

	7	7	4
+		6	4

e.

	3	3	4
+		8	2

f.

	5	7	1
+		7	6

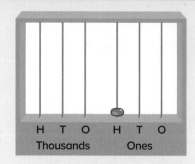

Step In   What number is shown on this abacus?

How does the value change if the bead is moved
to a rod on either side?

The value is 10 times **greater**
if moved one rod to the **left**. I
divide the value by 10 if the bead
is moved one rod to the **right**.

What does this chart show?

1,000 is 10 times greater
than 100, or 100 times
greater than 10. What
else do you notice?

Thousands			Ones		
H	T	O	H	T	O

×10   ×10   ×10   ×10   ×10

How would the value of each place change if you started at the left side of the
chart and moved to the right?

Step Up

1. Write **10**, **100**, or **1,000** to make each statement true.
   Use the above place-value chart to help your thinking.

a.

100,000 is _____ times greater than 10,000.

b.

1,000 is _____ times greater than 10.

c.

100,000 is _____ times greater than 1,000.

d.

10,000 is _____ times greater than 100.

2. Mechanical odometers start with all of the places at zero and change as the car travels. These odometers show the distance in miles that different cars have traveled. Write what the odometers would show if the cars travel more miles.

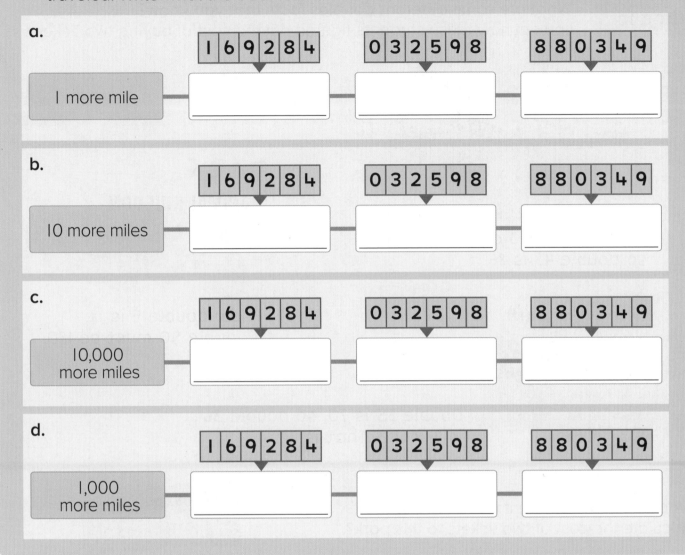

a.

1 6 9 2 8 4   0 3 2 5 9 8   8 8 0 3 4 9

I more mile

b.

1 6 9 2 8 4   0 3 2 5 9 8   8 8 0 3 4 9

10 more miles

c.

1 6 9 2 8 4   0 3 2 5 9 8   8 8 0 3 4 9

10,000 more miles

d.

1 6 9 2 8 4   0 3 2 5 9 8   8 8 0 3 4 9

1,000 more miles

Step Ahead

Lisa is acting in a movie. Her character is handed a briefcase that holds $100,000 in $100 bills. She opens the briefcase to check that the money is all there.

How many $100 dollar bills should be in the briefcase?

Working Space

Step In

What are some different doubles facts that you know?
Look at how these students figured out the cost of buying two tickets.

MOVIELAND $43

Double 40 is 80 and double 3 is 6, so double 43 is 86.

ANIMAL KINGDOM
$90   Admit One

I know double 9 is 18 so double 90 must be 180.

OCEAN WORLD $36

Double 35 is 70, so double 36 is 2 more. That is 72.

What are some different ways you could calculate the cost of two tickets to this park?

Water Wonderland
$24

Step Up

1. Calculate the cost of buying two of each item.

a.  $20

$ _____

b. $32

$ _____

c. $24

$ _____

d. 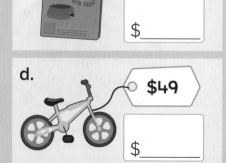 $49

$ _____

e. $23

$ _____

f.  $16

$ _____

2. Double these numbers. Write the products around the outside.

a.
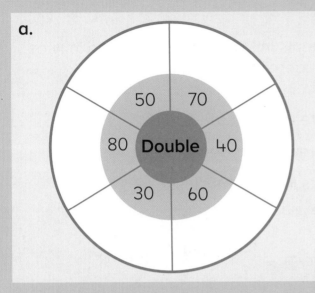

b.
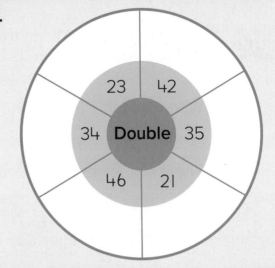

3. Write other two-digit numbers you can double in the pink boxes.
Then write the doubles in the blue boxes.

a.

× 2

b.
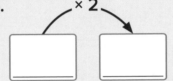
× 2

c.
× 2

d.
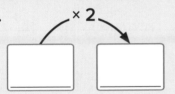
× 2

e.
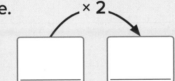
× 2

f.
× 2

Step Ahead   Solve each problem. Show your thinking.

a. Koda had $50. He bought
2 identical items and had $28
left. Which items did he buy?

b. Hannah bought 2 of the same
item. She spent $34. Which
items did she buy?

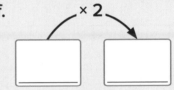

collar $24

leash $9

toys $11

DOG FOOD

brush $17

bowl $32

biscuits $43

Think and Solve **THINK TANK** the When the students in Megan's class line up in twos, there is one student left.

When they line up in threes, there is one student left.

When they line up in fives, there are no students left.

There are fewer than 30 students in Megan's class.

How many students are in Megan's class? [ ] students

Words at Work Write a word problem that involves multiplying a two-digit number by 2. Then write how you would solve the problem, and write an equation to show the solution.

_____

_____

_____

_____

_____

_____

_____

_____

_____

_____

_____

Ongoing Practice

I. Use real objects to help you complete this table. The base of each object is shaded.

Pyramids			
Number of faces			
Number of vertices			
Shape of base			
Number of sides on base			

2. Write numbers to make each statement true.

a.

10,000 is _____ times greater than 10.

b.

100,000 is _____ times greater than 1,000.

c.

1,000,000 is _____ times greater than 10,000.

Preparing for Module 2   Complete these statements.

a.
Half of 6 is ☐

SO

Half of 60 is ☐

b.
Half of 4 is ☐

SO

Half of 40 is ☐

c.
Half of 8 is ☐

SO

Half of 80 is ☐

d.
Half of 10 is ☐

SO

Half of 100 is ☐

Step In   Deon buys four bags of bread rolls.

How would you calculate the total number of rolls that he buys?

I can think double double. Double 6 is 12. Double 12 is 24. So 4 × 6 = 24.

What should you write in each box to show the total number of rolls?

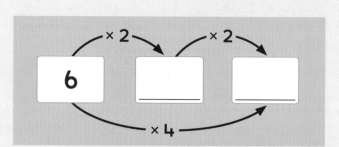

Use this diagram to calculate the total number of rolls in eight bags.

Why does this diagram look different from the diagram above?

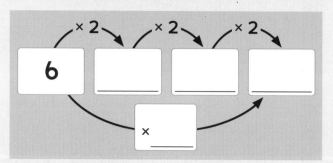

Step Up   I.   Use the doubles strategy to solve each problem.

a. There are 7 tins. Each tin holds 4 tennis balls. How many balls are there in total?

double __7__ is __14__

double __14__ is __28__ balls

b. There are 8 lengths of string. Each length is 8 inches long. What is the total length of the string?

double ____ is _____

double _____ is _____

double _____ is _____ inches

2. Complete each diagram.

a.
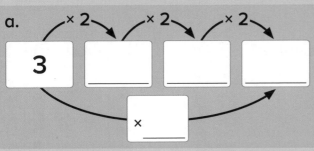

b.
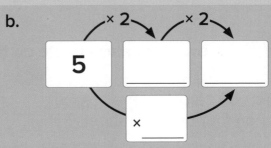

c.

×2   ×2

[8] [____] [____]

[____ × ____]

d.

×2   ×2   ×2

[9] [____] [____] [____]

[____ × ____]

3. Complete each fact. Then write the turnaround fact for each.

a.

$4 \times 9 =$ _____

____ × ____ = ____

b.

$8 \times 7 =$ _____

____ × ____ = ____

c.

$4 \times 6 =$ _____

____ × ____ = ____

4. Think about the fours and eights facts. Write the missing number in each equation.

a.

$3 \times 8 =$ [____]

b.

$56 =$ [____] $\times 8$

c.

$4 \times$ [____] $= 32$

d.

$4 = 4 \times$ [____]

e.

$8 \times$ [____] $= 16$

f.

[____] $= 8 \times 8$

g.

$12 = 4 \times$ [____]

h.

[____] $\times 4 = 16$

i.

$0 = 8 \times$ [____]

Step Ahead

Write the missing numbers.

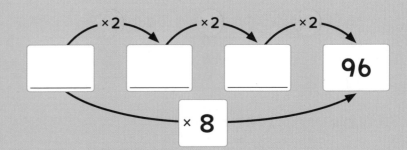

Step In

How many stickers are on this sheet?

STICKERS

How would you calculate the number of stickers on four of these sheets?

I can extend the double-double strategy. Double 24 is **48**. Double **48** is 96.

What should you write in this diagram to show the total number of stickers?

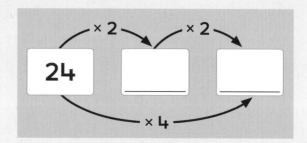

Andrea buys eight sheets of stickers.

How would you calculate the total numbers of stickers she buys?

Write numbers in each box to show your thinking.

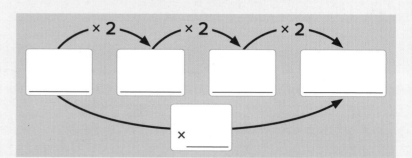

Step Up   I. Write the doubles. Then complete the equation.

a.
8 × 15 = ☐

Double 15 = 30

Double 30 = 60

Double 60 =

b.
4 × 12 = ☐

Double ___ = ___

Double ___ = ___

c.
8 × 25 = ☐

Double ___ = ___

Double ___ = ___

Double ___ = ___

© ORIGO Education

2. Complete each diagram. Show your thinking.

a.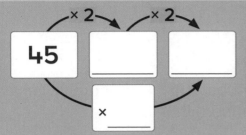

b.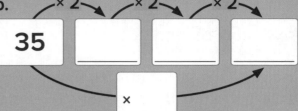

c.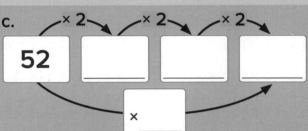

d.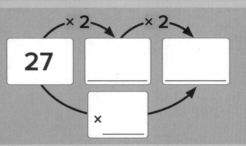

3. Write a number that is between 50 and 75 in each red box.
Then complete the diagrams. Show your thinking.

a.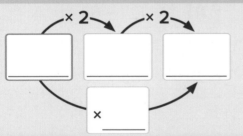

b.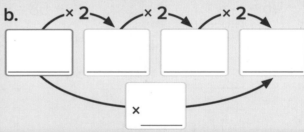

4. Complete each equation. Then write the turnaround. Show your thinking.

a.

$8 \times 75 =$ _____

_____ $\times$ _____ $=$ _____

b.

$4 \times 61 =$ _____

_____ $\times$ _____ $=$ _____

Step Ahead

Write in words how the doubles strategy can be extended to calculate 16×15.

_____

_____

_____

Computation Practice

★ Complete the equations. Then write each letter above its matching answer at the bottom of the page. Some letters appear more than once.

62 + 63 = ___ **i**	26 + 57 = ___ **p**	58 + 58 = ___ **t**
123 − 61 = ___ **w**	59 − 28 = ___ **r**	167 − 85 = ___ **y**
79 + 80 = ___ **o**	149 − 75 = ___ **n**	64 + 66 = ___ **b**
92 − 46 = ___ **l**	34 + 58 = ___ **m**	127 − 63 = ___ **u**
38 + 39 = ___ **h**	184 − 91 = ___ **s**	66 + 28 = ___ **e**
129 − 64 = ___ **z**		

125   116   125   93

125   92   83   159   93   93   125   130   46   94

116   159   93   74   94   94   65   94   62   125   116   77

82   159   64   31   94   82   94   93   159   83   94   74

Ongoing Practice

I. Calculate the perimeter of this shape. Show your thinking.

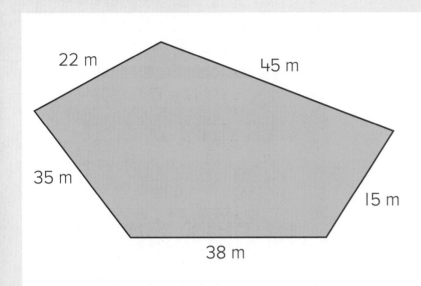

22 m

45 m

35 m

15 m

38 m

☐_____ m

2. Write the double and the double double.

a.
× 2   × 2

16 ☐_____ ☐_____

× 4

b.
× 2   × 2

45 ☐_____ ☐_____

× 4

c.
× 2   × 2

33 ☐_____ ☐_____

× 4

d.
× 2   × 2

17 ☐_____ ☐_____

× 4

Preparing for Module 2   Complete these equations.

a.
$20 = \boxed{} \times 4$

b.
$\boxed{} \times 5 = 0$

c.
$5 \times \boxed{} = 40$

d.
$\boxed{} = 5 \times 9$

e.
$5 \times 3 = \boxed{}$

f.
$50 = \boxed{} \times 10$

g.
$\boxed{} \times 5 = 30$

h.
$2 \times 5 = \boxed{}$

i.
$\boxed{} \times 7 = 35$

Step In   Write the product.

$7 \times 80 = \boxed{}$

What known multiplication fact helped you calculate the answer?

How does this equation match this picture of blocks?

$1 \times 17 = 17$

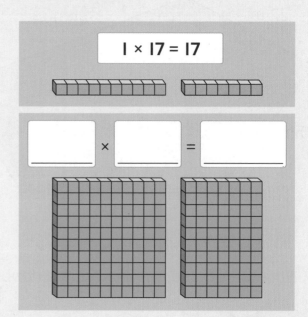

What equation would you write to match this picture of blocks?

$\boxed{} \times \boxed{} = \boxed{}$

What is the same about each equation?

What is different?

Complete each equation.

if ➤ $1 \times 17 = \boxed{}$

then ➤ $10 \times 17 = \boxed{}$

The second picture above has 10 times as many blocks.

How would you use the same strategy to calculate 10×24?

Step Up   1. Complete the multiplication fact. Then use the fact to calculate the product in each multiplication equation below.

a.
if ➤ $5 \times 7 = \boxed{}$

then ➤ $5 \times 70 = \boxed{}$

b.
if ➤ $4 \times 9 = \boxed{}$

then ➤ $4 \times 90 = \boxed{}$

c.
if ➤ $7 \times 6 = \boxed{}$

then ➤ $7 \times 60 = \boxed{}$

d.
if ➤ $6 \times 3 = \boxed{}$

then ➤ $6 \times 30 = \boxed{}$

2. Complete the first equation. Then use that to complete the second equation.

a.

if ➤ $1 \times 15 =$ ☐

then ➤ $10 \times 15 =$ ☐

b.

if ➤ $1 \times 25 =$ ☐

then ➤ $10 \times 25 =$ ☐

c.

if ➤ $1 \times 12 =$ ☐

then ➤ $10 \times 12 =$ ☐

d.

if ➤ $1 \times 39 =$ ☐

then ➤ $10 \times 39 =$ ☐

3. Complete each equation. Then write the turnaround for each.

a.
$9 \times 50 =$ _____

_____ × _____ = _____

b.
$40 \times 7 =$ _____

_____ × _____ = _____

c.
$10 \times 13 =$ _____

_____ × _____ = _____

d.
$18 \times 10 =$ _____

_____ × _____ = _____

e.
$10 \times 27 =$ _____

_____ × _____ = _____

f.
$8 \times 80 =$ _____

_____ × _____ = _____

Step Ahead This array shows 10×25. How could you use this array to help calculate 20×25? Complete the equations. Show your thinking.

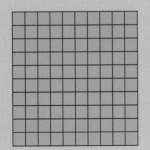 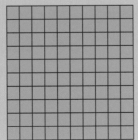 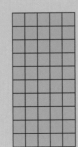

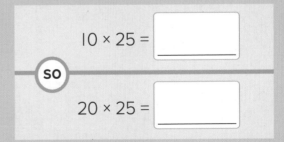

$10 \times 25 =$ ☐

so

$20 \times 25 =$ ☐

Step In

What is the same about these quantities? What is different?

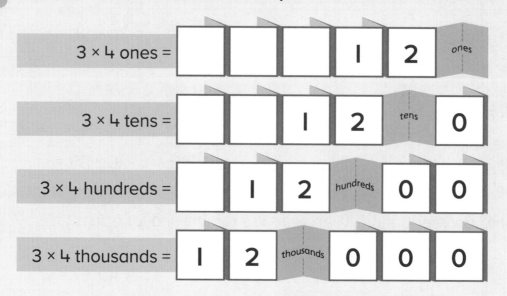

3 × 4 ones = [ ][ ][ ] 1 2 ones

3 × 4 tens = [ ][ ] 1 2 tens 0

3 × 4 hundreds = [ ] 1 2 hundreds 0 0

3 × 4 thousands = 1 2 thousands 0 0 0

What is another way to say the last three products?

What are the different ways you could say the products of these?

4 × 6 tens = ☐

4 × 6 hundreds = ☐

4 × 6 thousands = ☐

Step Up

1. Use a pattern to help you write the products.

a.
6 × 2 ones = 12 ones   **SO**   6 × 2 = 12

b.
6 × 2 tens = ☐ tens   **SO**   6 × 20 = ☐

c.
6 × 2 hundreds = ☐ hundreds   **SO**   6 × 200 = ☐

d.
6 × 2 thousands = ☐ thousands   **SO**   6 × 2,000 = ☐

2. Use a pattern to help you complete these equations.

a.

$9 \times 4 =$ ___

$9 \times 40 =$ ___

$9 \times 400 =$ ___

$9 \times 4,000 =$ ___

b.

$8 \times 9 =$ ___

$8 \times 90 =$ ___

$8 \times 900 =$ ___

$8 \times 9,000 =$ ___

c.

$7 \times 6 =$ ___

$70 \times 6 =$ ___

$700 \times 6 =$ ___

$7,000 \times 6 =$ ___

d.

$3 \times 7 =$ ___

$30 \times 7 =$ ___

$300 \times 7 =$ ___

$3,000 \times 7 =$ ___

3. Circle the multiplication facts that have the middle number as the product.

a.

12×20 60×4

240

3×80 400×6

b.

$4 \times 9,000$ 600×6

3,600

180×2 $3 \times 1,200$

Step Ahead   Write some pairs of numbers that multiply to make each product.

a.

2,800

b.

320

Think and Solve How can you use all three buckets to get exactly 20 L into the tub with the least possible number of pourings?

Buckets

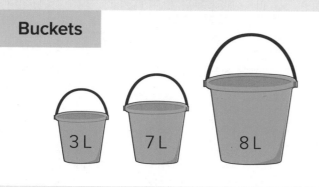

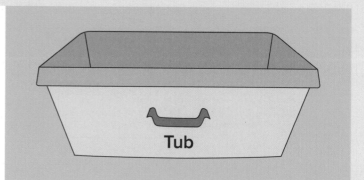

a. What is the least number of pourings? ☐

b. Write how you figured it out.

Words at Work Write about how you can use multiplication patterns to help you multiply numbers like 9 × 7,000.

© ORIGO Education

Ongoing Practice

1. The perimeter of this shape is 251 cm. Calculate the missing side length. Remember to show the unit. Show your thinking.

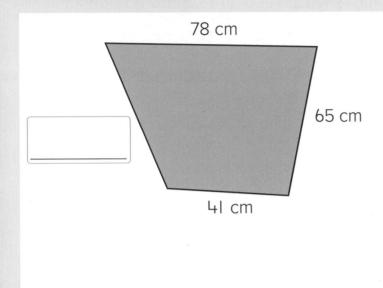

78 cm

65 cm

41 cm

2. Use a pattern to help complete these equations.

a.

$3 \times 4 =$ ____

$30 \times 4 =$ ____

$300 \times 4 =$ ____

$3{,}000 \times 4 =$ ____

b.

$9 \times 6 =$ ____

$90 \times 6 =$ ____

$900 \times 6 =$ ____

$9{,}000 \times 6 =$ ____

FROM 3.12.10

FROM 4.1.12

Preparing for Module 2   Complete these equations.

a. $90 =$ ____ $\times 10$

b. ____ $\times 9 = 0$

c. ____ $\times 8 = 72$

d. ____ $= 9 \times 6$

e. $9 \times 3 =$ ____

f. $36 =$ ____ $\times 9$

g. ____ $\times 5 = 45$

h. $2 \times$ ____ $= 18$

i. $9 \times 9 =$ ____

A sports club is planning to celebrate its 1,000,000th spectator. Each week, there are about 10,000 spectators at the game. The club estimates it has had about 474,000 attendees to date.

How many weeks is it until the club can celebrate the 1,000,000th spectator?
Show your thinking.

 Share why you chose this strategy.

ORIGO Stepping Stones · Grade 4 · Module 1

To play the game, darts are thrown at each target and the numbers are multiplied. Players have three chances to win. The first player to score the same product twice wins.

Luke says the top prize is impossible to win.
Giselle says it is possible to win.

Who do you agree with? Show your thinking.

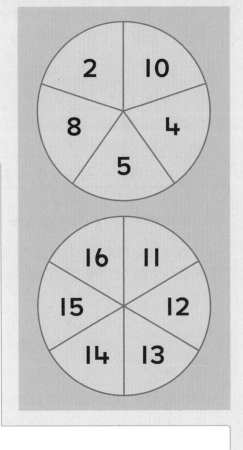

> I agree with ...
>
> I think this because ...

Share your thinking with another student. They can write their feedback below.

> I agree/disagree with your thinking because ...

Feedback from:

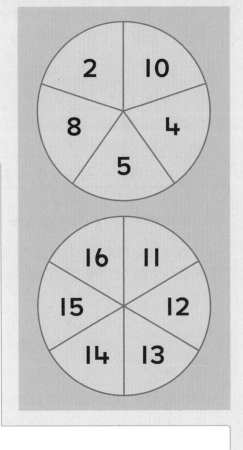 Discuss how the feedback you received will help you give better feedback to others.

Step In

This table shows the number of cars that drove past the northern entrance of a school in one week.

School Traffic Report – Northern Entrance							
	Sun	Mon	Tues	Wed	Thurs	Fri	Sat
Morning	195	395	354	398	405	589	217
Afternoon	235	354	409	376	437	630	289

About how many cars drove past the school on each school day?

Estimate the number of cars that drove past the school on Monday. How did you arrive at your estimate?

I looked for a nearby ten or hundred to round each number. I then added 400 + 350 = 750.

Estimate the number of cars that drove past the school on Friday. Is the total greater or less than 1,000? How did you decide?

There were more than 500 cars in the morning and in the afternoon, so the total has to be greater than 1,000.

Step Up

1. Look at the table above. Estimate the total number of cars for each of these days. Show your thinking.

a.   Wednesday

Estimate _____

b.   Thursday

Estimate _____

c.   Tuesday

Estimate _____

d.   Saturday

Estimate _____

This table shows the number of cars that drove past the southern entrance of a school in one week.

School Traffic Report – Southern Entrance							
	Sun	Mon	Tues	Wed	Thurs	Fri	Sat
Morning	127	278	305	288	414	354	185
Afternoon	204	252	349	291	394	340	109

2. Write the day on which the total number of cars that drove past the school is closest to each number below. Show your thinking.

a. About 800 cars

Day: _____

b. About 700 cars

Day: _____

c. About 300 cars

Day: _____

d. About 600 cars

Day: _____

Step Ahead

Look at the table above. Estimate the total number of cars driven past the school in the mornings. Show your thinking.

Estimate [_____] cars

2.2 Addition: Reviewing the standard algorithm (composing tens)

Step In What does this table show?

How could you calculate the total attendance on Saturday?

Theater Attendance		
	Saturday	Sunday
Morning	74	67
Afternoon	115	125

I can figure that out in my head …
115 + 70 = 185   185 + 4 = 189

How could you calculate the total attendance on Sunday?

Hunter used the standard addition algorithm. He followed these steps.

Step 1	Step 2	Step 3	Step 4
H T O	H T O	H T O	H T O
1 2 5	1 2 5	1 2 5	1 2 5
+ 6 7	+ 6 7	+ 6 7	+ 6 7
	2	9 2	1 9 2

What did Hunter do in each step?

What does the red digit in the tens column mean?

What is another way to add these numbers?

The standard algorithm is useful when the numbers are difficult to add.

Step Up 1. Estimate each total. Then use the standard addition algorithm to calculate the exact total.

a.
Estimate _____

```
    4  5  8
+  2  1  4
```

b.
Estimate _____

```
    2  5  3
+  1  3  8
```

c.
Estimate _____

```
    2  0  9
+     4  5
```

d.
Estimate _____

```
    4  2  8
+  2  6  2
```

Theater Attendance					
	Monday	Tuesday	Wednesday	Thursday	Friday
Morning	56	109	127	118	87
Afternoon	125	132	45	115	108

2. Use the table above. Estimate the total attendance for each day in your head. Then use the standard addition algorithm to calculate the exact total.

a.
Estimate for Monday _____

	1	2	5
+		5	6

b.
Estimate for Tuesday _____

	1	3	2
+	1	0	9

c.
Estimate for Wednesday _____

	1	2	7
+		4	5

d.
Estimate for Thursday _____

e.
Estimate for Friday _____

Step Ahead   Write the digit that is missing in each box. Regroup if necessary.

a.

	3	1	3
+	2	4	9
	5		2

b.

	1	5	8
+	4	0	9
	5		7

c.

	6	0	7
+			9
	6	8	6

d.

	1		6
+	8	1	7
	9	9	3

Computation Practice

★ For each division fact, write the multiplication fact you would use to help calculate the quotient. Then write the quotients. Complete the facts as fast as you can. Use the classroom clock to time yourself.

Time Taken:

start

$54 \div 9 =$ ☐

☐ $\times$ ☐ $=$ ☐

$30 \div 6 =$ ☐

☐ $\times$ ☐ $=$ ☐

$48 \div 6 =$ ☐

☐ $\times$ ☐ $=$ ☐

$24 \div 3 =$ ☐

☐ $\times$ ☐ $=$ ☐

$36 \div 9 =$ ☐

☐ $\times$ ☐ $=$ ☐

$45 \div 9 =$ ☐

☐ $\times$ ☐ $=$ ☐

$15 \div 3 =$ ☐

☐ $\times$ ☐ $=$ ☐

$36 \div 6 =$ ☐

☐ $\times$ ☐ $=$ ☐

$54 \div 6 =$ ☐

☐ $\times$ ☐ $=$ ☐

$21 \div 3 =$ ☐

☐ $\times$ ☐ $=$ ☐

$72 \div 9 =$ ☐

☐ $\times$ ☐ $=$ ☐

$81 \div 9 =$ ☐

☐ $\times$ ☐ $=$ ☐

$27 \div 3 =$ ☐

☐ $\times$ ☐ $=$ ☐

$42 \div 6 =$ ☐

☐ $\times$ ☐ $=$ ☐

finish

$18 \div 3 =$ ☐

☐ $\times$ ☐ $=$ ☐

$63 \div 9 =$ ☐

☐ $\times$ ☐ $=$ ☐

Ongoing Practice

1. Complete the missing parts.

a.

126,309

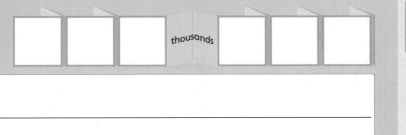

thousands

b.

four hundred fourteen thousand one hundred sixty-nine

thousands

2. Estimate each total. Show your thinking.

a. 287 + 589

Estimate _____

b. 408 + 235

Estimate _____

c. 395 + 217

Estimate _____

Preparing for Module 3

Write these numbers in order from **least** to **greatest**.

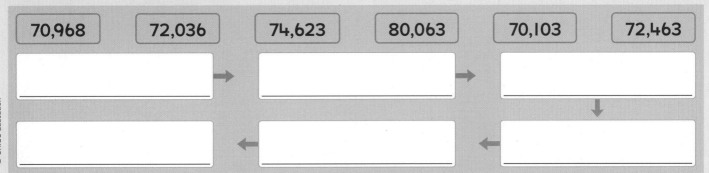

| 70,968 | 72,036 | 74,623 | 80,063 | 70,103 | 72,463 |

Addition: Reviewing the standard algorithm (composing hundreds)

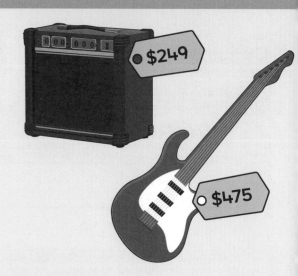

$249

$475

Step In	How could you calculate the total cost of these two items?

These numbers are difficult to add mentally, so I would use a written method to calculate the total.

Monique used the standard addition algorithm to calculate the total.

What steps did she follow?

What does each 1 above the 4 and 7 mean?

What is another way to add these numbers?

	1	1	
	4	7	5
+	2	4	9
	7	2	4

What steps would you follow to calculate 535 + 196?

Write the missing numbers.

	5	3	5
+	1	9	6

Step Up	1. Estimate each total. Then use the standard addition algorithm to calculate the exact total.

a.

Estimate _____

	5	3	4
+	2	8	6

b.

Estimate _____

	4	8	3
+		3	6

c.

Estimate _____

	2	7	3
+		7	8

d.

Estimate _____

	3	4	8
+	2	9	5

Fundraising								
Class	2A	2B	3A	3B	4A	4B	5A	5B
Money	$108	$268	$282	$227	$197	$345	$386	$435

2. Use the table above. Estimate in your head the total money raised by each grade level. Then use the standard addition algorithm to calculate the exact total.

a. Grade 2

b. Grade 3

c. Grade 4

d. Grade 5

3. Use your answers in Question 2 to help you calculate these totals.

a. Grades 2 and 3 $_____

b. Grades 2 and 4 $_____

Step Ahead

Correct the error in this calculation. Then describe the mistake in words.

	4	8	1
+	3	7	5
	7	5	6

Step In	What does this table show?

How could you calculate the total drinks sold in Week 1?

Drink Sales		
	Week 1	Week 2
Juice	614	857
Milk	531	435

Carter used blocks to represent the sales from each type of drink. He then moved the blocks together to calculate the total.

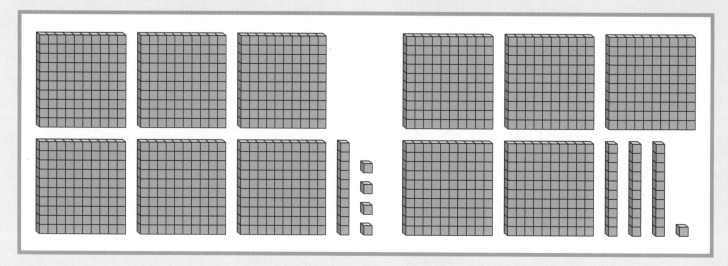

What number do all the blocks show? How do you know?

What is another way to represent the same number?

> I could regroup 10 hundreds blocks as 1 thousands block.

How could you calculate the total drinks sold in Week 2?

Karen used the standard addition algorithm to calculate the total.

What numbers should she write to complete the calculation?

```
      ¹
    8 5 7
  + 4 3 5
  ───────
      9 2
```

Karen adds 8 and 4.

She writes the total (12) in the empty space.

What does the 12 actually represent?

Step Up

Hot Food Sales					
	Week 1	Week 2	Week 3	Week 4	Week 5
Veggie Burger	1,205	748	915	1,324	1,201
Grilled Chicken Sandwich	1,317	1,055	1,230	1,197	997

Estimate the total sales for each week in your head.
Then use the standard addition algorithm to calculate the exact total.

a. Week 1 total

```
    1 | 3 | 1 | 7
+   1 | 2 | 0 | 5
```

b. Week 2 total

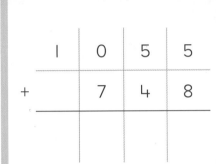

```
    1 | 0 | 5 | 5
+       7 | 4 | 8
```

c. Week 3 total

```
    1 | 2 | 3 | 0
+       9 | 1 | 5
```

d. Week 4 total [＿＿＿]

e. Week 5 total [＿＿＿]

Step Ahead

Use the totals above to help calculate these totals.

a. Total sales in Weeks 1 and 2

[＿＿＿]

b. Total sales in Weeks 3 and 5

[＿＿＿]

Think and Solve   THINK TANK

The sum of four different odd numbers is 34.

The least number is 5.

The difference between the least number and the greatest number is 8.

a. What are the four numbers?

b. Write how you figured it out.

Words at Work

Write about when you or someone you know needs to estimate a total outside of school. Write at least three sentences to describe your example.

I. Write the matching number on the expander.
Then write the number in words.

a.

| 4 hundred thousands |
| I ten thousand |

_____

_____

b.

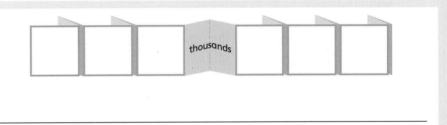

| 9 hundred thousands |
| 6 ten thousands |

_____

_____

2. For each of these, use the standard addition algorithm to calculate the total cost.

a.

| H | T | O |

\+

b.

| H | T | O |

\+

c.

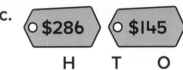

| H | T | O |

\+

Preparing for Module 3   Round each population to the nearest **hundred**.

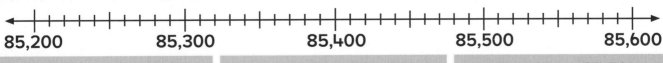

85,200   85,300   85,400   85,500   85,600

a. Population **85,289**

_____

b. Population **85,405**

_____

c. Population **85,564**

_____

Step In   What does this table show?

How could you calculate the total downloads for Hip Hop Anthems and Sisters of Soul?

It is a bit hard to remember all the numbers, so I would use a written method to figure out the total.

Music Downloads	
Album Title	Downloads
Dance Mix	12,395
Country Classics	10,080
Hip Hop Anthems	8,451
Sisters of Soul	3,243

Ramon used the standard addition algorithm to calculate the total.

What steps has he done already?

Write the numbers to complete the calculation.

What does the 11 actually represent?

		8	4	5	1
+		3	2	4	3
			6	9	4

How could you calculate the total downloads for Dance Mix and Country Classics?

I know the total will be about 22,500.

Show how you could use the standard algorithm to calculate the total.

Step Up
1. Estimate each total. Then use the standard addition algorithm to calculate the exact total.

a. Estimate

	9	5	7	3
+	5	2	0	6

b. Estimate

	2	3	0	7	2
+		4	2	9	3

c. Estimate

	4	0	8	5	4
+	1	0	2	3	7

Movie Downloads				
	January	February	March	April
Rocking Robots	23,059	47,630	124,276	152,609
Dancing Dinos	14,237	25,273	125,802	74,305

2. Estimate the total downloads for each month.
Then use the standard addition algorithm to calculate the exact total.

a.

January estimate _____

b.

February estimate _____

c.

March estimate _____

d.

April estimate _____

Step Ahead Estimate the number of downloads for each movie.
Then calculate the exact total for each. Show your thinking.

Rocking Robots	Dancing Dinos
Estimate _____	Estimate _____
Exact total _____	Exact total _____

Step In

This table shows the number of games sold in each of three years.

How would you estimate the total games sold in these three years?

I rounded the number sold for each year to the nearest thousand.

Space Race	
Year	Number Sold
2014	935
2015	1,210
2016	742

How could you check your estimate?

How could you calculate the exact total sales?

Julia used the standard addition algorithm to calculate the total.

Does it matter in what order she writes the numbers to add?

What steps did she follow?

Is her answer correct? If not, write the changes she should make.

	1	2	1	0
		9	3	5
+		7	4	2
	1	8	8	7

Step Up

I. Estimate each total. Then use the standard addition algorithm to calculate the exact total.

a. Estimate

		8	0	4
		3	9	6
+		2	7	5

b. Estimate

	1	4	5	2	0
		3	0	7	4
+		1	2	0	9

c. Estimate

	3	2	0	8	0
	1	4	5	2	5
+		2	4	7	3

Game Sales			
	Battleships	Grow a Garden	Dino Attack
2014	805	13,600	117,290
2015	15,320	11,275	120,095
2016	10,160	8,032	110,910

2. Use the table above. Estimate in your head the total sales for each game.
Then use the standard addition algorithm to calculate the exact total.

a. Battleships	b. Grow a Garden	c. Dino Attack

3. Calculate the total sales for each year. Show your thinking.

a. 2014	b. 2015	c. 2016

Step Ahead

Write the missing digits to show correct totals. Write the
regrouping digits that are missing to help your thinking.

a.
```
    5 [ ]  3  0
      3  4 [ ]
  +   1  2  6
  ─────────────
    5  8  9  7
```

b.
```
    6  0  7  1
  [ ]  7  0  1
  +   3  2  5
  ─────────────
    9 [ ] 9  7
```

c.
```
  [ ]   5  1  8
    4  2 [ ] 0
  +  1  0  2  7
  ─────────────
  [ ]  2  7  4  5
```

© ORIGO Education

Computation Practice

If Samuru stood facing south with his back to the north, what would be on his left hand?

★ Complete the equations. Then write each letter above its matching answer at the bottom of the page. Some letters appear more than once.

$220 + 350 =$ ___	**o**	$670 - 350 =$ ___	**e**
$760 - 240 =$ ___	**n**	$260 + 520 =$ ___	**u**
$510 + 330 =$ ___	**s**	$790 - 450 =$ ___	**a**
$560 - 340 =$ ___	**h**	$210 + 460 =$ ___	**d**
$450 + 310 =$ ___	**i**	$970 - 420 =$ ___	**b**
$580 - 170 =$ ___	**g**	$240 + 530 =$ ___	**r**
$350 + 140 =$ ___	**m**	$650 - 410 =$ ___	**f**
$780 - 430 =$ ___	**t**		

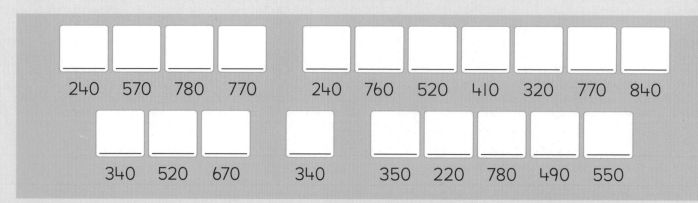

240   570   780   770   240   760   520   410   320   770   840

340   520   670   340   350   220   780   490   550

Ongoing Practice

1. Calculate the total cost. Write an equation to show your thinking.

a.

| ○ 75¢ | ○ 55¢ |

Total $____ and ____¢

b.

| ○ 20¢ | ○ 65¢ | ○ 35¢ |

Total $____ and ____¢

2. Estimate each total in your head. Then use the standard addition algorithm to calculate the exact total.

a.

3	6	0	9
+		3	4	5

b.

2	1	6	7
+ 3	4	8	5

c.

7	5	6	0
+ 1	7	5	9

d.

2	1	0	3	9
+ 1	6	9	8	0

Preparing for Module 3

Double one number and halve the other. Then write the products.

a.
$15 \times 6 =$ _____

is the same value as

____ × ____ = ____

b.
$35 \times 6 =$ _____

is the same value as

____ × ____ = ____

c.
$3 \times 22 =$ _____

is the same value as

____ × ____ = ____

d.
$32 \times 5 =$ _____

is the same value as

____ × ____ = ____

e.
$18 \times 5 =$ _____

is the same value as

____ × ____ = ____

f.
$8 \times 45 =$ _____

is the same value as

____ × ____ = ____

Step In

An online store sold 12,098 cell phones in January and 9,810 cell phones in February. In March, 500 more cell phones were sold than in January.

What is your estimate of the total number of sales for January, February, and March?

How did you arrive at your estimate?

How would you calculate the total sales for March and February?

I will call the number of sales in March M and the total number of sales T.
M = 12,098 + 500, and T = 9,810 + M.

The store planned to sell 25,000 cell phones from January to March.
How many more cell phones have to be sold to reach this target?
What is your estimate?

Step Up

1. Write an equation to represent each problem. Use a letter to represent the unknown amount. You do not need to calculate the final answers.

a. Dwane buys 2 cell phones. Each phone costs $395. He then pays an extra $50 for insurance. What is the total amount he pays?

b. Natalie sends 186 text messages in June and another 249 in July. She makes only 35 calls during this time. How many text messages did she send in total over the two months?

c. In May, Corey received twice as many text messages as he sent. He sent 152 text messages. How many text messages did he receive?

d. Fatima buys a cell phone and a tablet. The tablet costs $780, which is $150 more than the cell phone. How much did the cell phone cost?

2. Solve each problem. Show your thinking.

a. There were 940 fewer laptops sold than cell phones sold. There were 1,807 laptops sold. How many cell phone were sold?

```
  1
1,807
+ 940
 2747
```

2,747 cell phones

b. The record number of cell phones sold over a 12 month period is 1,089. Gloria beat the record by 94 sales. How many cell phones did she sell?

```
 1 1
1,089
+  94
1,183
```

1,183 cell phones

c. 35,408 people were surveyed. 11,340 males have cell phones. 2,875 more females have cell phones than males. How many females have cell phones?

```
  1 1
11,340
+ 2,875
14,215
```

14,215 females

d. 6,309 phone chargers were sold in 2015. Twice as many phone chargers were sold in 2016. How many cell phone chargers were sold in 2016?

```
   1
 6,309
+6,309
12,618
```

12,618 chargers

| **Step Ahead** | Use these numbers to write an addition word problem. | 8,302   11,915   291 |

Jena baked 291 cookies in May. 8,302 more cookies were made in June, and 11,915. in July. How many cookies did she bake in all 3 months?

Step In   What number do these blocks show?

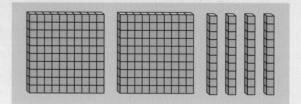

How could you halve this number?

Complete this statement.

Half of 240 is [ ]

The blocks can be shared between two groups. That is 1 hundred and 2 tens each.

How would you calculate half of this number?

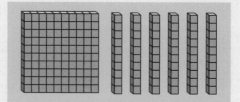

I can show the same number with 16 tens. That is 8 tens each.

Or I could think of a double. $2 \times ? = 160$.

What strategy would you use to calculate half of 130?

What double could be used to help your thinking?

Step Up   1. Complete each statement. Use blocks to help your thinking.

a.
    Double 230 is [ ]

b.
    Half of 260 is [ ]

c.
    Half of 420 is [ ]

d.
    Double 120 is [ ]

2. Complete each statement. Show your thinking.

a.

Half of 140 is [   ]

b.

Double 90 is [   ]

c.

Double 150 is [   ]

d.

Half of 230 is [   ]

3. Double or halve each number. Show your thinking.

a.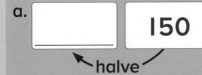

[   ] **150** halve

b.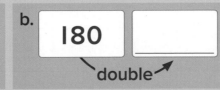

180 [   ] double

c.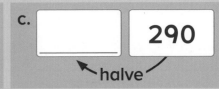

[   ] **290** halve

Step Ahead

Liam has 2 one-dollar bills, 2 quarters, 3 dimes, and 2 nickels. He spends half his money at the store. How much money does he have left? Show your thinking.

$[   ] and [   ]¢

Think and Solve

Amy bought 2 books for $36.

One book cost twice as much as the other.

What did each book cost? $24, $12

Words at Work

Research populations of towns in your state. Write about three places that have a population greater than 10,000, but less than 100,000.

Estimate the total of the three populations, then explain the method you would use to find the exact total.

© ORIGO Education

Ongoing Practice

1. Color the bills and coins that you would use to pay the exact price. No change will be given.

○ **$7 and 37¢**

2. Double or halve each number. Show your thinking.

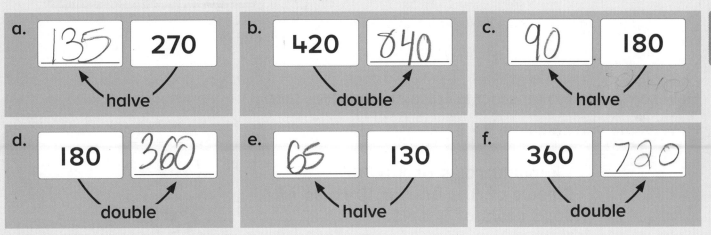

a. 135 → **270** halve

b. **420** → 840 double

c. 90 → **180** halve

d. **180** → 360 double

e. 65 → **130** halve

f. **360** → 720 double

Preparing for Module 3

Use multiplication to help you calculate the total area of each large rectangle.

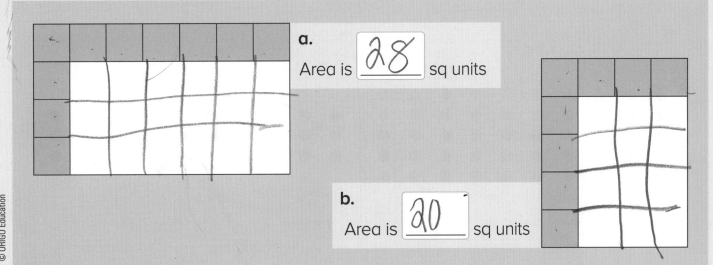

a. Area is 28 sq units

b. Area is 20 sq units

Step In

What tens facts could you write to match this array?

$$\boxed{} \times \boxed{} = \boxed{}$$
$$\boxed{} \times \boxed{} = \boxed{}$$

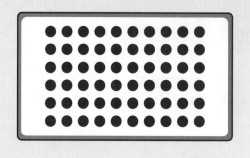

How would you calculate the product?

Terri makes a fives fact by covering half the number of dots.

What fives fact could you write to match this array?

$$\boxed{} \times \boxed{} = \boxed{}$$
$$\boxed{} \times \boxed{} = \boxed{}$$

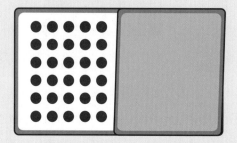

How can you use a tens fact to calculate any fives fact?

How would you calculate 9 × 5?

I know 10 rows of 9 is 90.
5 rows of 9 is half of 10 rows of 9.
So, 5 rows of 9 is 45.

Step Up

I. Complete the tens fact. Circle half the array and then complete the fives facts to match.

a.

5 × 10 = ◻

5 × 5 = ◻

b.

3 × 10 = ◻

3 × 5 = ◻   5 × 3 = ◻

2. Complete the tens fact. Circle half the array and then complete the two
fives facts to match.

a.

$7 \times 10 =$ ☐

☐ × ☐ = ☐

☐ × ☐ = ☐

b.

$4 \times 10 =$ ☐

☐ × ☐ = ☐

☐ × ☐ = ☐

c.

$8 \times 10 =$ ☐

☐ × ☐ = ☐

☐ × ☐ = ☐

3. Write the tens fact that you would use to help calculate the fives fact.
Then complete the fives fact.

a.

$6 \times 5 =$ ☐

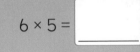

$6 \times 10 = 60$

b.

$9 \times 5 =$ ☐

☐ × ☐ = ☐

Step Ahead

Reece and Lillian each have 90 cents. Lillian has only dimes and
Reece has only nickels. They decide to put their coins into one pile.
How many coins do they have in total? Show your thinking.

☐ coins

Step In

A bricklayer is laying a path. It is 5 bricks wide and 28 bricks long. How many bricks will be needed?

I don't know 28 × 5, but I do know 28 × 10.

28 × 10 = 280 and a **half of 280 = 140**
So, **28 × 5 = 140**

How could you use the same strategy to calculate these?

16 × 5 = ____

44 × 5 = ____

25 × 5 = ____

34 × 5 = ____

Step Up

1. Use the same strategy to complete these.

a.
24 × 10 = 240

one-half of 240 is 120

so

24 × 5 = 120

b.
16 × 10 = ____

one-half of ____ is ____

so

16 × 5 = ____

2. Use the first equation to help you calculate the second equation.

a.
$15 \times 10 =$ ____

so

$15 \times 5 =$ ____

b.
$48 \times 10 =$ ____

so

$48 \times 5 =$ ____

c.
$18 \times 10 =$ ____

so

$18 \times 5 =$ ____

d.
$64 \times 10 =$ ____

so

$64 \times 5 =$ ____

e.
$42 \times 10 =$ ____

so

$42 \times 5 =$ ____

f.
$32 \times 10 =$ ____

so

$32 \times 5 =$ ____

3. Complete each equation. Show your thinking.

a.
$26 \times 5 =$ ____

b.
$35 \times 5 =$ ____

c.
$68 \times 5 =$ ____

Step Ahead   Solve each problem. Show your thinking.

a. A soccer coach buys 5 team shirts and 5 pairs of shorts. Shirts cost $35, shorts cost $17, and socks cost $9. How much money does she spend?

$ ____

b. Ruth earns $18 an hour. Chayton earns $24 an hour. If they each work 5 hours, what is the difference between the amounts they earn?

$ ____

Computation Practice

★ Write each total in the puzzle grid below.

Across	Down
a. 200 + 15 + 30	**a.** 200 + 56 + 30
c. 200 + 53 + 40	**b.** 500 + 28 + 30
e. 500 + 57 + 30	**c.** 200 + 44 + 30
f. 600 + 48 + 30	**d.** 300 + 34 + 20
h. 400 + 64 + 20	**g.** 700 + 28 + 50
j. 300 + 55 + 30	**i.** 800 + 66 + 10
l. 100 + 34 + 30	**j.** 300 + 71 + 20
n. 700 + 25 + 40	**k.** 500 + 56 + 20
o. 100 + 36 + 40	**l.** 100 + 22 + 30
p. 200 + 45 + 10	**m.** 400 + 65 + 20

I. **a.** Use the grid lines to draw three different rectangles.

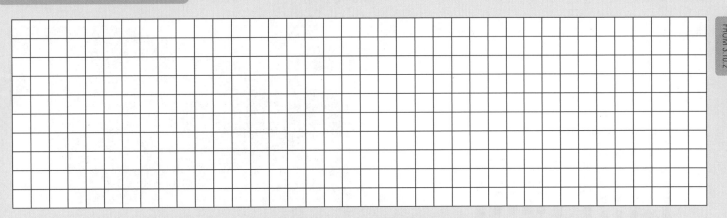

FROM 3.10.2

b. In each rectangle you drew, write the area in square units (sq units).

c. Write **G** inside the rectangle with the **greatest** area.

d. Write **L** inside the rectangle with the **least** area.

2. Complete these.

a.

18 × 10 = ____

one-half of ____ is ____

(SO)

18 × 5 = ____

b.

62 × 10 = ____

one-half of ____ is ____

(SO)

62 × 5 = ____

FROM 4.2.10

Preparing for Module 3

Use the centimeter rulers to calculate the perimeter of this rectangle. Show your thinking.

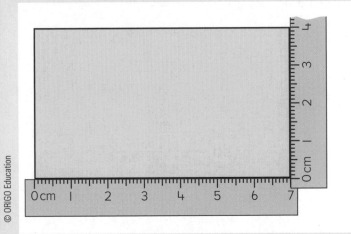

Perimeter is ____

Step In

There are **9** rows of carrots. There are **4** carrots in each row. How many carrots are there in total?

How did you calculate the product?

Jamar used a tens multiplication fact to help calculate the answer.

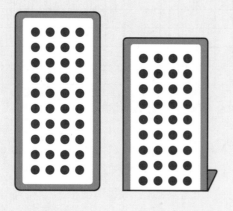

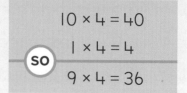

$$10 \times 4 = 40$$
$$1 \times 4 = 4$$
SO
$$9 \times 4 = 36$$

10 rows of 4 is 40.
9 rows of 4, is 4 less.
9 rows of 4 is 36.

How does his strategy help to calculate the answer?

Would this strategy work for all nines facts?

How could you use this strategy to calculate 9 × 7?

Step Up

1. Use the same strategy to calculate these.

a.
$$10 \times 3 = \boxed{30}$$
$$1 \times 3 = \boxed{3}$$
SO
$$9 \times 3 = \boxed{27}$$

b.
$$10 \times 6 = \boxed{}$$
$$1 \times 6 = \boxed{}$$
SO
$$9 \times 6 = \boxed{}$$

c.
$$10 \times 8 = \boxed{}$$
$$1 \times 8 = \boxed{}$$
SO
$$9 \times 8 = \boxed{}$$

2. Write the product for the tens fact. Then use that fact to help you write the nines fact and its turnaround.

a.
10 × 5 = ☐

SO

9 × 5 = ____

5 × 9 = ____

b.
10 × 7 = ☐

SO

____ × ____ = ____

____ × ____ = ____

c.
10 × 4 = ☐

SO

____ × ____ = ____

____ × ____ = ____

d.
10 × 2 = ☐

SO

____ × ____ = ____

____ × ____ = ____

e.
10 × 6 = ☐

SO

____ × ____ = ____

____ × ____ = ____

f.
10 × 8 = ☐

SO

____ × ____ = ____

____ × ____ = ____

3. Write the missing number in each fact.

a. 9 × 3 = ☐

b. 9 × ☐ = 18

c. 81 = ☐ × 9

d. 9 = 9 × ☐

e. ☐ × 9 = 63

f. 0 = 9 × ☐

Step Ahead   Use the tens fact to complete each equation.

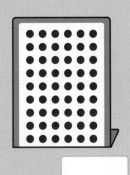

9 × 6 = ☐

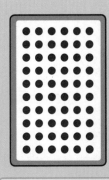

10 × 6 = 60

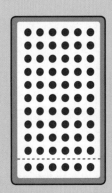

11 × 6 = ☐

Step In

There are nine rows of seats. There are 17 seats in each row. How many seats are there in total?

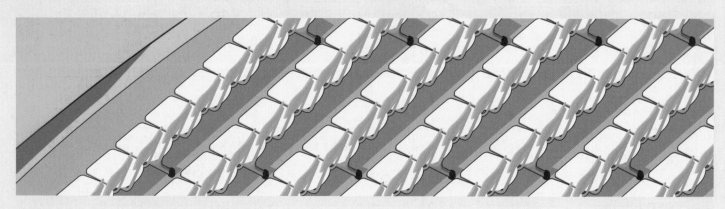

How did you calculate the total?

I extended the nines strategy. 10 rows of 17 is 170. So, 9 rows of 17 must be 17 less — that is 153.

Complete each sentence to calculate **9 × 17.**

Why do you subtract one row of 17?

What happens if you decide to add one row of 17?

It costs $19 to buy one shirt.
How could you use a method similar to that above to calculate the cost of buying three shirts?

What nearby fact could you use to help?

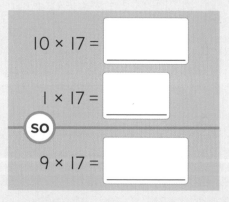

$10 \times 17 = \boxed{}$

$1 \times 17 = \boxed{}$

SO

$9 \times 17 = \boxed{}$

Step Up   I.   Use the same strategy to complete these.

a.
$10 \times 14 = \boxed{140}$

$1 \times 14 = \boxed{14}$

SO

$9 \times 14 = \boxed{126}$

b.
$10 \times 19 = \boxed{}$

$1 \times 19 = \boxed{}$

SO

$9 \times 19 = \boxed{}$

c.
$10 \times 12 = \boxed{}$

$1 \times 12 = \boxed{}$

SO

$9 \times 12 = \boxed{}$

2. Use a nearby fact to complete each of these.

a.

$30 \times 5 =$ ___

$1 \times 5 =$ ___

SO

$29 \times 5 =$ ___

b.

$40 \times 2 =$ ___

$1 \times 2 =$ ___

SO

$39 \times 2 =$ ___

c.

$20 \times 4 =$ ___

$1 \times 4 =$ ___

SO

$19 \times 4 =$ ___

d.

___ $\times$ ___ $=$ ___

___ $\times$ ___ $=$ ___

SO

$39 \times 4 =$ ___

e.

___ $\times$ ___ $=$ ___

___ $\times$ ___ $=$ ___

SO

$19 \times 3 =$ ___

3. Complete each equation. Show your thinking.

a.

$29 \times 4 =$ ___

b.

$9 \times 15 =$ ___

c.

$9 \times 35 =$ ___

Step Ahead Calculate the total cost of each cell phone plan.

a. Selena pays $29 each month for her cell phone plan. How much will she pay over 6 months?

$ ___

b. Connor pays $45 a month for his cell phone plan. How much will he pay over 9 months?

$ ___

Think and Solve

Read the clues and look at the map.
Write the matching letter for each town.

Clues

- The distance from Eastwood to Franklin and back is 170 km.

- The distance from Eastwood to Lynnfield and back is 120 km.

- Milton is 97 km from Franklin.

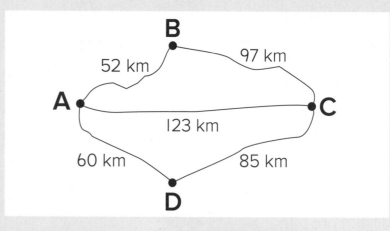

Eastwood ____

Milton ____

Lynnfield ____

Franklin ____

Words at Work

Imagine another student was away from school when you learned about extending the nines multiplication strategy. Write how you would explain the strategy to them.

_____

_____

_____

_____

_____

_____

_____

_____

_____

_____

Ongoing Practice

1. New carpet is needed in these rooms. Calculate the area of each floor plan. Show your thinking.

a.

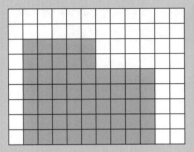

Area is [ ] sq units

b.

Area is [ ] sq units

FROM 3.10.5

2. Use a tens fact to complete each of these.

a.
$10 \times 12 =$ [ ]

$1 \times 12 =$ [ ]

SO

$9 \times 12 =$ [ ]

b.
$10 \times 15 =$ [ ]

$1 \times 15 =$ [ ]

SO

$9 \times 15 =$ [ ]

c.
$10 \times 14 =$ [ ]

$1 \times 14 =$ [ ]

SO

$9 \times 14 =$ [ ]

FROM 4.2.12

Preparing for Module 3

Solve each problem. Show your thinking. Remember to show the correct unit.

a. A square tile has a perimeter of 16 inches. What is the area of the tile?

b. A rectangular floor has an area of 20 square yards. It is 5 yards long. What is its perimeter?

Kevin, Deana, and Mike are playing the same online game as a team. The team score is 585 points. Together, Deana and Kevin have 15 fewer points than Deana's and Mike's combined score. Kevin has the least score, and Mike has the greatest score.

How many points could each player have? Show your thinking.

 Share another real-world situation where you could use similar thinking.

At a bake sale, Logan's cupcakes are 2 for $9, and Kay's cupcakes are $5 each. At the end of the sale, Logan and Kay have made the same amount of money. Each person has made more than $50.

2 for $9

$5 each

How many cupcakes could each person have sold? Show your thinking.

Logan has sold _____ cupcakes and Kay has sold _____ cupcakes.

I know my answers work because ...

_____

_____

_____

_____

_____

_____

_____

Share your thinking with another student. They can write their feedback below.

I agree/disagree with your thinking because ...

Feedback from:

_____

_____

_____

_____

Discuss how the feedback will help you improve the feedback you give.

Step In

These tables show the populations* of ten cities.

City	Population
Billings, MT	110,263
Cary, NC	159,769
Everett, WA	108,010
Fargo, ND	118,523
Green Bay, WI	105,207

City	Population
Lansing, MI	115,056
McKinney, TX	162,898
Palm Bay, FL	107,888
Springfield, MA	154,341
Sunnyvale, CA	151,754

*2015 US Census Bureau estimate

How can you figure out which city has the greatest population?

Which city has the least population?

Does Springfield or McKinney have the greater population?

How could you use this number line to help you decide?

100,000   200,000

Which cities have a population that is greater than 120,000?

How can you figure it out? What helps you decide?

I looked at the digit in the ten thousands place.

Step Up

1. Write the population of each city. Then write **<** or **>** to complete each sentence. You can use the number line to help your thinking.

a. Sunnyvale ◯ Lansing

b. Billings ◯ Fargo

c. Everett ◯ Palm Bay

d. McKinney ◯ Cary

This table shows the populations* of another six cities.
Use this table for Questions 2 to 4.

City	Population
Cape Coral, FL	175,229
Charleston, SC	132,609
Sioux Falls, SD	171,544
High Point, NC	110,268
Kansas City, KS	151,306
Lafayette, LA	127,657

*2015 US Census Bureau estimate

2. a. Which city has the **greatest** population?

b. Which city has the **least** population?

3. Write the population of each city. Then write **<** or **>** to complete each sentence.

a. Charleston ◯ Sioux Falls

b. Kansas City ◯ Cape Coral

c. High Point ◯ Sioux Falls

d. Lafayette ◯ Charleston

e. Charleston ◯ Cape Coral

f. Kansas City ◯ High Point

4. Write the city names in order from **least** to **greatest** population.

Step Ahead

Look at the population table at the top of this page.
Which cities have a population that is **greater** than 110,000
but **less** than 150,000?

Step In

Blake is watching some friends play a video game.

They ask him to quickly record the number of points that they each score.

Which player has the greatest number of points? How did you decide?

Morgan	41,207
Jacob	8,950
Antonio	45,712
Dorothy	100,060

 The places are not lined up, so I will have to think carefully about the value of each digit.

How could you compare the number of points that Morgan and Antonio scored?

Which digits would you look at to help you decide who has more?

Complete each statement to compare the points that Morgan and Antonio scored.

[____] > [____]   [____] < [____]

Step Up

1. Write each player's score.
   Then write **<** or **>** to make a true statement.

a.
   Morgan [____] ◯ Jacob [____]

b.
   Jacob [____] ◯ Dorothy [____]

c.
   Antonio [____] ◯ Dorothy [____]

d.
   Dorothy [____] ◯ Morgan [____]

© ORIGO Education

The highest scores of another six players are recorded on this notepad.
Use these scores to complete Questions 2 to 4.

Jie	90,529
Susan	107,315
Jerome	9,059
Rita	104,901
Robert	60,000
Amber	10,470

2. a. Who has the most points?

b. Who has the fewest points?

3. Write each player's score. Then write **<** or **>** to complete each sentence.

a. Susan ⬡ Jerome

b. Robert ⬡ Jie

c. Rita ⬡ Jerome

d. Amber ⬡ Rita

e. Jerome ⬡ Jie

f. Susan ⬡ Rita

4. Write each player's score in order from **greatest** to **least**.

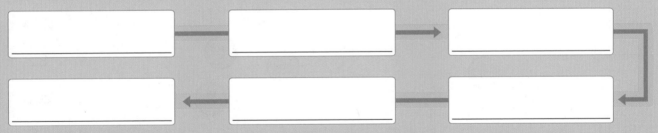

Step Ahead

Patricia has more points than both Ben and Amy.
Matthew has more points than Amy, but fewer points than Ben.

Who has the lowest score?

Computation Practice

Does the ocean say anything to the beach?

★ Use a ruler to draw a straight line to each correct product. The line will pass through a number and a letter. Then write each letter above its matching number at the bottom of the page.

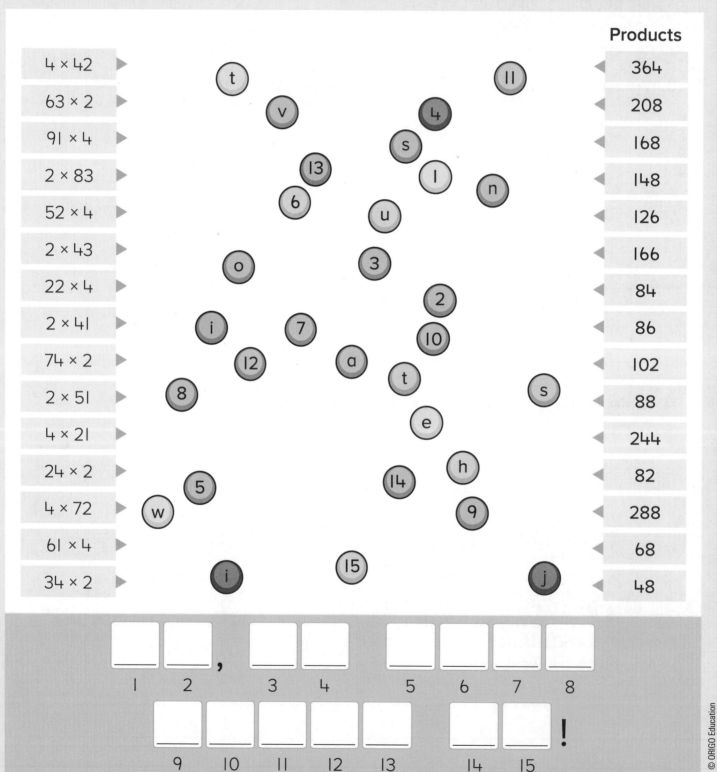

Products

4 × 42 ▶

63 × 2 ▶

91 × 4 ▶

2 × 83 ▶

52 × 4 ▶

2 × 43 ▶

22 × 4 ▶

2 × 41 ▶

74 × 2 ▶

2 × 51 ▶

4 × 21 ▶

24 × 2 ▶

4 × 72 ▶

61 × 4 ▶

34 × 2 ▶

◀ 364
◀ 208
◀ 168
◀ 148
◀ 126
◀ 166
◀ 84
◀ 86
◀ 102
◀ 88
◀ 244
◀ 82
◀ 288
◀ 68
◀ 48

_1 _2 , _3 _4 _5 _6 _7 _8

_9 _10 _11 _12 _13 _14 _15 !

© ORIGO Education

1. Estimate each total. Then use the standard addition algorithm to calculate the exact total.

FROM 4.2.4

a.
Estimate

```
    1  6  1  5
+   1  4  7  2
_____
```

b.
Estimate

```
    2  4  8  6
+   1  3  7  3
_____
```

c.
Estimate

```
    2  1  0  8
+   2  0  9  5
_____
```

2. Write these populations in order from **greatest** to **least**.

City	Population
Boston	645,966
Denver	649,495
Nashville	659,042
El Paso	674,433
Memphis	653,450
Washington	658,893

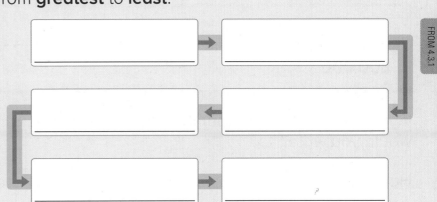

FROM 4.3.1

Estimate the **difference** between these lengths. Then write an equation to show your thinking.

a.

| 68 cm | 95 cm |

The difference is about _____ cm.

b.

| 83 cm | 35 cm |

The difference is about _____ cm.

Step In This table shows the annual home game attendance totals for some NFL teams.

Which team had the greatest total attendance?

Which teams had a total of more than 630,000 spectators?

Team	Total
Dallas	704,345
NY Giants	641,184
Green Bay	623,577
Washington	617,767
NY Jets	615,656

Which teams had about 620,000 spectators?

How can you figure this out? Which digits will you look at to help you decide?

Draw an arrow on this number line to show the total attendance at the NY Giants' home games.

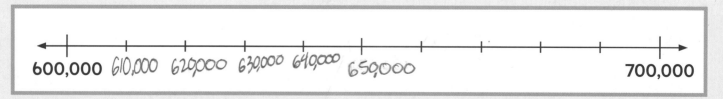

If you had to round this number to the nearest **hundred thousand,** what number would you write? 600,000

How would you round the same number to the nearest **ten thousand?** 640,000

Step Up Use the table and number line above to help you complete these.

1. Round the total attendance for these teams to the nearest **hundred thousand.**

   a. Dallas 700,000 ✓   b. NY Giants 600,000 ✓

2. Round the total attendance for these teams to the nearest **ten thousand.**

   a. NY Jets 620,000 ✓   b. Green Bay 620,000 ✓

3. Round the total attendance for these teams to the nearest **thousand.**

   a. Washington 618,000 ✓   b. Dallas 704,000 ✓

This table shows the annual home game attendance totals for some other NFL teams. Use this table for Questions 4 to 7.

Team	Total
Seattle	545,577
Chicago	498,864
New England	550,048
Denver	614,977
Houston	573,271

4. Which teams had a total of more than 550,000 spectators attend their home games?

New England, Denver, and Houston ✓

5. Round the total attendance for these teams to the nearest **hundred thousand**.

a. Houston 60,0000 ✓
b. New England 600,000 ✓

6. Round the total attendance for these teams to the nearest **ten thousand**.

a. Denver 610,000 ✓
b. Seattle 550,000 ✓

7. Round the total attendance for these teams to the nearest **thousand**.

a. Chicago 499,000 ✓
b. New England 550,000 ✓

8. Round each number to the nearest **ten**, **hundred**, and **thousand**.

	Nearest Ten	Nearest Hundred	Nearest Thousand
432,068	432,070 ✓	432,100 ✓	432,000 ✓
809,506	809,510 ✓	809,500 ✓	810,000 ✓
565,271	565,270 ✓	565,300 ✓	565,000 ✓

Step Ahead

Write the number that is closest to 250,000. Use each digit once.

301,569 ✓

    5 3 9 0 1 6

Step In The table shows the monthly number of visitors to a popular monument.

June	142,309
July	110,050
August	151,782
September	97,612

How would you estimate the total number of visitors?

C.T.

Rounding the number of monthly visitors can make it easier to add.

Can you think of some other situations where rounding might be useful?

Paige decides to round the number of visitors in September to the nearest hundred.

Which digits should she look at to help her round the number?

I looked at the digit in the hundreds place, and the digit with the next lowest place value. 97,612. The number is rounded down to 97,600.

How could you use a number line to help round the number?

Step Up Use the table at the top of the page to complete these.

1. Round the number of visitors in each month to the nearest **thousand**.

   a. September 98,000   b. June 142,000

2. Round the number of visitors in each month to the nearest **hundred thousand**.

   a. July 100,000   b. August 200,000

This table shows the monthly number of visitors to a museum.

January	9,403
February	27,513
March	103,470
April	86,089

3. Round the number of visitors in each month to the nearest **ten thousand**.

a. April   90,000

b. February   30,000

4. Round the number of visitors in each month to the nearest **hundred**.

a. March   103,500

b. January   9,400

5. Round the number of visitors in each month to the nearest **ten**.

a. April   80,090

b. February   27,510

6. Explain how you would round the number of visitors in January to the nearest **thousand**.

First, I would see the hundreds place, 4. Then I know 4 is below 5, so we would round down. Keep the 9, and change everything else into a zero. 9,000

Step Ahead

Use rounding to estimate the total number of visitors to the museum above. Write the numbers you decided to add in the space below. Then write your estimate.

✓ • ✗

```
  11
103,500   March
 90,000   April
 30,000   February
+ 9,400   January
232,900
```

232,900 visitors

Think and Solve

THINK TANK

Dakota has 12 more cards than Yasmin.
Norton has 3 fewer cards than Arleen.

a.
How many cards does each ☐ represent?

_____

b.
Who has 18 fewer cards than Joel?

_____

Arleen	☐	☐	☐	☐	☐	☐		
Norton	☐	☐	☐	☐	☐			
Yasmin	☐	☐						
Dakota	☐	☐	☐	☐				
Joel	☐	☐	☐	☐	☐	☐	☐	☐

Words at Work

Write how you could figure out possible scores for Steven and Sharon.

When Steven's highest score is rounded to the nearest hundred, it is less than when it is rounded to the nearest thousand. When Sharon's highest score is rounded to the nearest thousand, it is less than when it is rounded to the nearest hundred. Both scores have the same digit in the ten thousands and the thousands places.

_____

_____

_____

_____

_____

_____

_____

_____

_____

_____

Ongoing Practice

I. Estimate each total. Then use the standard addition algorithm to calculate the exact total.

a.

Estimate _____

	2	6	1	8
+	1	2	6	5

b.

Estimate _____

	4	6	5	7
+	3	7	0	2

c.

Estimate _____

	3	2	8	9
+	2	0	1	5

2. Round each population to the nearest **hundred**.

a. Population 423,156

b. Population 213,308

c. Population 239,279

d. Population 344,120

e. Population 632,051

f. Population 302,015

g. Population 431,076

h. Population 547,329

i. Population 102,418

Preparing for Module 4

Estimate each difference. Then use the standard subtraction algorithm to calculate the exact difference.

a.

Estimate _____

	6	2	3
−	3	0	7

b.

Estimate _____

	5	3	3
−	2	0	9

c.

Estimate _____

	7	8	2
−	4	1	9

d.

Estimate _____

	3	1	2
−	1	0	9

Step In   Imagine you start at 1,000 and skip count by 1,000.

What number will you say after 999,000?

Have you heard the word **millions** being used before?
How much is one million?

Look at the place-value chart below.

What place names belong in the three spaces below **Millions**?

Write the missing abbreviations in the boxes.

One million pennies stacked on top of one another would reach almost a mile into the sky!

Millions			Thousands			Ones		
			H	T	O	H	T	O

Write numbers in the chart to show one million.

How could you represent one million using different base-10 blocks?

How many ones blocks would you need? How many tens blocks?
How many hundreds blocks? What pattern would you see?

Step Up   1. Imagine you had base-10 blocks of each size. Write the missing numbers. Then complete the matching equations.

A **millions** block could be regrouped as

_____ hundred thousands	_____ × _____	=	1,000,000
_____ ten thousands	_____ × _____	=	1,000,000
_____ thousands	_____ × _____	=	1,000,000
_____ hundreds	_____ × _____	=	1,000,000
_____ tens	_____ × _____	=	1,000,000
_____ ones	_____ × _____	=	1,000,000

2. Color the ⬭ for the answer that makes sense.

a. The distance from Dallas to Detroit is about ...

⬭ 1,000,000 miles   ⬭ 100,000 miles   ⬭ 1,000 miles

b. The population of Austin, Texas is about ...

⬭ 1,000,000 people   ⬭ 100,000 people   ⬭ 1,000 people

c. The height of a skyscraper is about ...

⬭ 1,000,000 feet   ⬭ 100,000 feet   ⬭ 1,000 feet

3. Write **10**, **100**, or **1,000** to make each statement true.

a. 1,000,000 is [_____] times greater than 100,000.

b. 10,000 is [_____] times greater than 100.

c. 100,000 is [_____] times greater than 10,000.

d. 1,000,000 is [_____] times greater than 1,000.

e. 10,000 is [_____] times greater than 1,000.

Step Ahead   Write the number of bills you could trade for $1,000,000.

a.
_____

b.
_____

c.
_____

d.
_____

e.
_____

f.
_____

Step In

How many squares are in each row of this number chart?

Start at 5 and write the numbers as you count in steps of five. What pattern do you see?

These numbers are called **multiples** of 5.

Color all the squares that will show a multiple of 2. How did you decide?

Write all the multiples of 6 in the correct squares on the chart. What do you notice about these numbers?

	2		5	6

Look at the diagram on the right.

Write 24 in the first box.
What numbers could you write in the second box so the relationship is true?

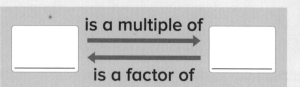

is a multiple of

is a factor of

A factor must divide the other number exactly. What does the diagram tell you about the numbers you wrote?

Step Up

I. Write numbers to complete these.

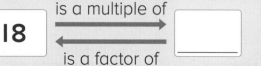
a.
18
is a multiple of
is a factor of

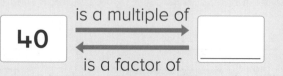
b.
40
is a multiple of
is a factor of

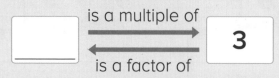
c.
is a multiple of
3
is a factor of

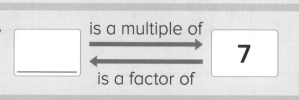
d.
is a multiple of
7
is a factor of

2. Choose numbers from the box at the top to complete the three diagrams below. Some numbers are not used. Each number is used only once.

a.

40	35	5	4	56
8	15	7	28	20

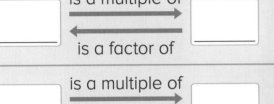

is a multiple of →
← is a factor of

is a multiple of →
← is a factor of

is a multiple of →
← is a factor of

b.

72	16	85	14	15
17	18	48	84	75

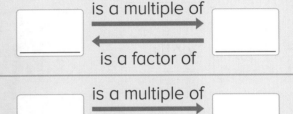

is a multiple of →
← is a factor of

is a multiple of →
← is a factor of

is a multiple of →
← is a factor of

3. Write **true** or **false**. Show your thinking.

a. 17 is a multiple of 3

b. 30 is a multiple of 6

c. 8 is a factor of 38

Step Ahead

② ③ ④ ⑤ ⑥ ⑦ ⑧ ⑨

These counters are placed in a bag. Three students take out one counter each. They then skip count by their number to 100.

The teacher notices that all three students say the numbers 45 and 90. Draw the counters they had.

Computation Practice   **What horse never wears a saddle?**

★ Complete the equations. Find each difference in the grid below and cross out the letter above. Then write the remaining letters at the bottom of the page.

360 – 179 = **481**	420 – 159 = **261**	510 – 389 = **121**
620 – 279 = **341**	720 – 239 = **481**	380 – 299 = **81**
520 – 369 = **151**	680 – 389 = **291**	720 – 469 = **251**
360 – 289 = **71**	530 – 179 = **351**	670 – 499 = **171**
730 – 589 = **141**	440 – 169 = **271**	460 – 369 = **91**
560 – 499 = **61**	630 – 149 = **481**	760 – 179 = **581**

Write the remaining letters in order from the ✳ to the bottom-right corner.

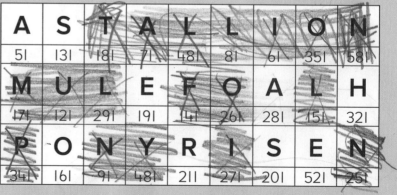

A	S	T	A	L	L	I	O	N
51	131	181	71	481	81	61	351	581
M	U	L	E	F	O	A	L	H
171	121	291	191	141	261	281	151	321
P	O	N	Y	R	I	S	E	N
341	161	91	481	211	271	201	521	251

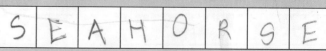

A   S E A H O R S E

© ORIGO Education

Ongoing Practice

1. Estimate each total. Then use the standard addition algorithm to calculate the exact total.

FROM 4.2.6

a.

Estimate ____ ☐

```
  4  3  6  0
     8  0  4
+    2  7  3
_____
```

b.

Estimate ____ ☐

```
  3  6  0  2  0
     2  6  5  4
+    1  1  6  8
_____
```

c.

Estimate ____ ☐

```
  5  2  7  8  9
  1  3  5  4  0
+    3  4  2  0
_____
```

2. Write numbers to complete each of these.

FROM 4.3.6

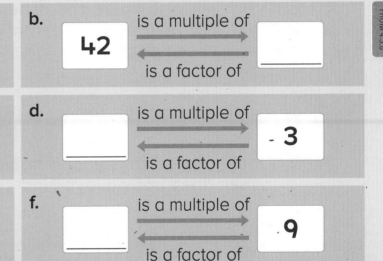

a. 24 — is a multiple of → ☐ / ← is a factor of

b. 42 — is a multiple of → ☐ / ← is a factor of

c. ☐ — is a multiple of → 5 / ← is a factor of

d. ☐ — is a multiple of → · 3 / ← is a factor of

e. 30 — is a multiple of → ☐ / ← is a factor of

f. ☐ — is a multiple of → 9 / ← is a factor of

Preparing for Module 4

Estimate each difference. Then use the standard subtraction algorithm to calculate the exact difference.

a.

Estimate ____ ☐

```
  2  5  7
- 1  4  7
_____
```

b.

Estimate ____ ☐

```
  6  1  2
- 4  3  6
_____
```

c.

Estimate ____ ☐

```
  5  3  1
-    7  5
_____
```

d.

Estimate ____ ☐

```
  8  1  0
- 4  0  3
_____
```

Step In   What do you notice about the arrays?

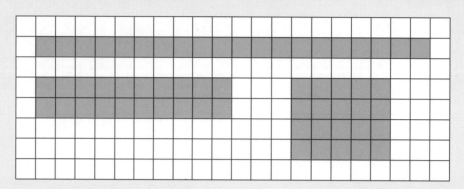

Complete this table to describe each array.

What do you notice about the factors?

You can double one factor and halve the other to help find different pairs of factors.

20
is the same value as
_____ × _____
_____ × _____
_____ × _____

How could you figure out all the factors of 18?

Doubling one factor and halving the other does not always find every factor.

Step Up   1.   Write all the factors of each number.

a.   **32**
is the same value as

_____ × _____

_____ × _____

_____ × _____

b.   **12**
is the same value as

_____ × _____

_____ × _____

_____ × _____

c.   **28**
is the same value as

_____ × _____

_____ × _____

_____ × _____

d.   **16**
is the same value as

_____ × _____

_____ × _____

_____ × _____

2. Write all the factors of each number.

a.   42
is the same value as

___ × ___

___ × ___

___ × ___

___ × ___

b.   30
is the same value as

___ × ___

___ × ___

___ × ___

___ × ___

c.   24
is the same value as

___ × ___

___ × ___

___ × ___

___ × ___

d.   64
is the same value as

___ × ___

___ × ___

___ × ___

___ × ___

e.   48
is the same value as

___ × ___

___ × ___

___ × ___

___ × ___

f.   36
is the same value as

___ × ___

___ × ___

___ × ___

___ × ___

g.   80
is the same value as

___ × ___

___ × ___

___ × ___

___ × ___

h.   100
is the same value as

___ × ___

___ × ___

___ × ___

___ × ___

Step Ahead

This array shows 2 × 15. How could you cut and rearrange it to show 6 × 5? Color the array to show the cuts you would make. Then write the steps that you would follow.

Step In Color an array to represent each of these numbers.

19   5   23

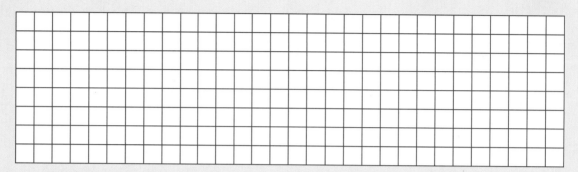

What do you notice?

What are some other **prime numbers** that you know?

What are some **composite numbers** that you know?

How could you prove that a number is composite?

> A **prime number** is any whole number greater than zero that has exactly two unique factors – itself and one.
>
> A **composite number** is a whole number that has more than two whole number factors.

A composite number can be represented by an array that has more than one equal row.

Step Up I. Color all the composite numbers.
Then color a matching array to prove that each number is composite.

 13

 9

 16

 2

 25

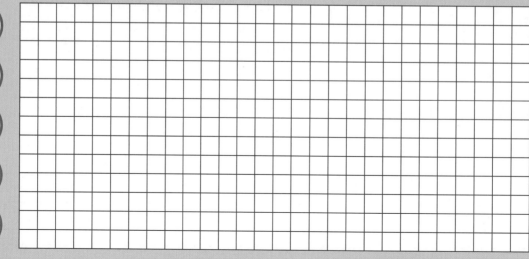

2. Look at this chart.

a. Circle the number 2. Draw a \ through all the multiples of 2. What do you notice?

1	2	3	4	5	6
7	8	9	10	11	12
13	14	15	16	17	18
19	20	21	22	23	24
25	26	27	28	29	30
31	32	33	34	35	36
37	38	39	40	41	42
43	44	45	46	47	48
49	50	51	52	53	54
55	56	57	58	59	60
61	62	63	64	65	66
67	68	69	70	71	72
73	74	75	76	77	78
79	80	81	82	83	84
85	86	87	88	89	90
91	92	93	94	95	96
97	98	99	100	101	102
103	104	105	106	107	108
109	110	111	112	113	114
115	116	117	118	119	120

b. Circle the number 3. Draw a / through all the multiples of 3. What do you notice?

c. Find the multiples of 6. What do you notice?

d. Circle the number 5.
Cross out all the multiples of 5.

e. Circle the number 7.
Cross out all the multiples of 7.

f. Choose three numbers that have not been crossed out. What are their factors?

Step Ahead Write 2 prime numbers greater than 120.

Think and Solve · THINK TANK

a. Who took the most time to travel to school?

_____

b. How long did that person take?

_____

- Sandra left home at 6:50 a.m.
  She arrived at school at 7:15 a.m.

- Emilio left home at 7:05 a.m.
  He arrived at school at 7:26 a.m.

- Olivia left home at 7:00 a.m.
  She arrived at school at 7:28 a.m.

Words at Work

Write a two-digit prime number and a two-digit composite number.

Prime	Composite

Write how you know your numbers are prime and composite.

_____

_____

_____

_____

_____

_____

_____

_____

_____

_____

_____

1. Use the standard subtraction algorithm to calculate the difference. Remember to estimate the answer to check that it makes sense.

FROM 3.9.6

a.
H	T	O
2	6	5
− 1	8	2

b.
H	T	O
4	0	5
− 2	6	8

c.
H	T	O
7	4	8
− 6	0	4

2. Write all the factors of each number.

FROM 4.3.7

a. 18
is the same value as

___ × ___

___ × ___

___ × ___

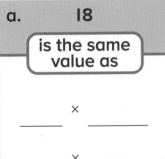

b. 50
is the same value as

___ × ___

___ × ___

___ × ___

c. 32
is the same value as

___ × ___

___ × ___

___ × ___

d. 40
is the same value as

___ × ___

___ × ___

___ × ___

Solve each problem. Show your thinking.

a. Carmela walked 319 steps to school. Hiro walked 147 steps to the same school. What is the difference between the distances?

_____ steps

b. There are 38 fewer students in Grade 3 than Grade 4. There are 206 students in Grade 4. How many students are in Grade 3?

_____ students

Step In

Each small square in this large rectangle measures 1 yard by 1 yard.

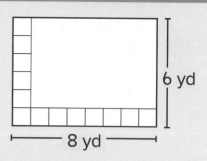

6 yd

8 yd

What are the dimensions of the large rectangle?

The width is 6 yards.
The length is 8 yards.

How could you use the dimensions to calculate the area of the rectangle?

A short way to write square units is to use a small 2. For example, 370 square yards can be written as 370 yd^2.

Does the order in which you multiply matter? Explain.

What rule could you write to calculate the area of any rectangle?

Use your rule to calculate the area of a rectangle that is 7 yards wide and 9 yards long.

Step Up

1. Imagine that each small square inside these large rectangles measures 1 yd by 1 yd. Write the dimensions of the whole rectangle. Then write how you will use the dimensions to calculate the area.

a.

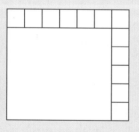

Length _____ yd   Width _____ yd

_____

_____

Area _____ yd^2

b.

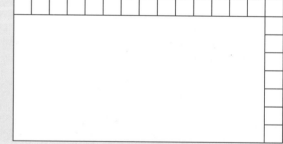

Length _____ yd   Width _____ yd

_____

_____

Area _____ yd^2

2. Calculate the area of each rectangle. Show your thinking.

a.

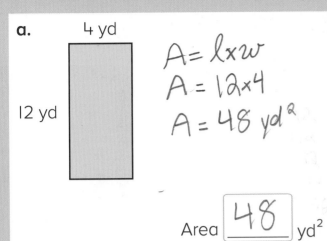

4 yd

12 yd

$A = l \times w$
$A = 12 \times 4$
$A = 48 \text{ yd}^2$

Area ___48___ yd²

b.

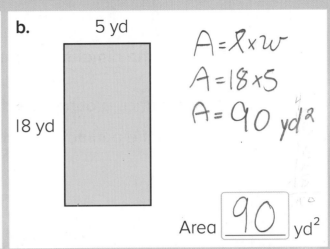

5 yd

18 yd

$A = l \times w$
$A = 18 \times 5$
$A = 90 \text{ yd}^2$

Area ___90___ yd²

3. Write possible dimensions for each rectangle.

a.

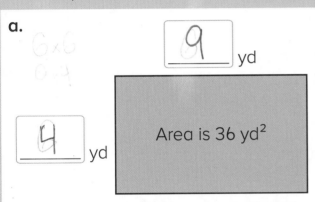

___9___ yd

___4___ yd

Area is 36 yd²

b.

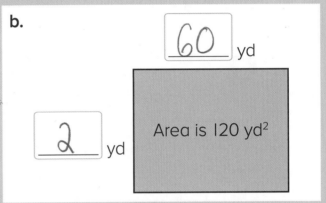

___60___ yd

___2___ yd

Area is 120 yd²

4. Write how you figured out each dimension in Question 3.

I thought of all the problems that equal to the tota area. :) :) :) :) :) :) :)

Step Ahead   Calculate the area of this rectangle.

Area ___207___ yd²

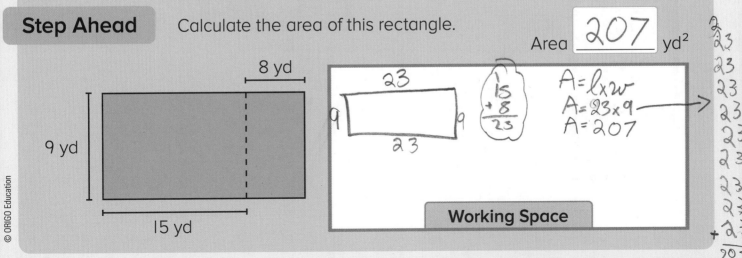

8 yd

9 yd

15 yd

23

9   15
       + 8
9   23

23

$A = l \times w$
$A = 23 \times 9$
$A = 207$

23
23
23
23
23
23
23
23
23
23
+ 23
_____
207

Working Space

© ORIGO Education

Step In

What are the dimensions of this mirror frame?

What do you call the distance around a rectangle?

How could you calculate the perimeter of this mirror frame?

12 + 12 + 6 + 6 = 36 inches

What is another way you could calculate the perimeter?

You could multiply the length and width by 2. Then add them together. That is 2 × 12 + 2 × 6.

12 in

6 in

What rule could you write to calculate the perimeter of a rectangle?

Step Up

I. Calculate the perimeter of each frame.

a.

18 in

9 in

2 × 18 = ☐

2 × 9 = ☐

Perimeter _____ in

b.

7 in

15 in

2 × 7 = ☐

2 × 15 = ☐

Perimeter _____ in

2. Calculate the perimeter of these. Show your thinking.

a.

12 in

18 in

$P = 2 \cdot (l + w)$
$P = 2 \cdot (18 + 12)$
$P = 2 \cdot (30)$
$P = 60$

Perimeter ⟨60⟩ in

b.

15 in

21 in

$P = 2 \cdot (l + w)$
$P = 2 \cdot (21 + 15)$
$P = 2 \cdot (36)$
$P = 72$

Perimeter ⟨72⟩ in

3. Calculate the perimeter of each rectangle. Show your thinking.

a. Length is 15 in. Width is 8 in.

$P = 2 \cdot (l + w)$
$P = 2 \cdot (15 + 8)$
$P = 2 \cdot (23)$
$P = 46$

Perimeter ⟨46⟩ in

b. Length is 25 in. Width is 16 in.

$P = 2 \cdot (l + w)$
$P = 2 \cdot (25 + 16)$
$P = 2 \cdot (41)$
$P = 82$

Perimeter ⟨82⟩ in

Step Ahead

Calculate the perimeter of each polygon. For each shape, all sides are the same length.

a.

6 in

Perimeter ⟨24⟩ in

b.

9 in

Perimeter ⟨27⟩ in

c.

5 in

Perimeter ⟨30⟩ in

3.10 Maintaining concepts and skills

Computation Practice

★ For each division fact, write the multiplication fact you would use to help you calculate the answer. Then write the answers. Use the classroom clock to time yourself.

Time Taken:

start

$72 \div 8 =$ ☐ ☐ × ☐ = ☐

$14 \div 2 =$ ☐ ☐ × ☐ = ☐

$40 \div 8 =$ ☐ ☐ × ☐ = ☐

$36 \div 4 =$ ☐ ☐ × ☐ = ☐

$20 \div 5 =$ ☐ ☐ × ☐ = ☐

$32 \div 4 =$ ☐ ☐ × ☐ = ☐

$16 \div 4 =$ ☐ ☐ × ☐ = ☐

$24 \div 4 =$ ☐ ☐ × ☐ = ☐

$18 \div 2 =$ ☐ ☐ × ☐ = ☐

$12 \div 6 =$ ☐ ☐ × ☐ = ☐

$48 \div 8 =$ ☐ ☐ × ☐ = ☐

$28 \div 4 =$ ☐ ☐ × ☐ = ☐

$32 \div 8 =$ ☐ ☐ × ☐ = ☐

$16 \div 2 =$ ☐ ☐ × ☐ = ☐

finish

$14 \div 7 =$ ☐ ☐ × ☐ = ☐

$56 \div 8 =$ ☐ ☐ × ☐ = ☐

$24 \div 8 =$ ☐ ☐ × ☐ = ☐

◆ 110

ORIGO Stepping Stones · Grade 4 · 3.10

1. Estimate each difference. Then use the standard subtraction algorithm to calculate the exact difference.

FROM 3.9.6

a.

Estimate

_____

H	T	O
6	4	5
– 3	8	2

b.

Estimate

_____

H	T	O
7	6	1
– 2	4	9

c.

Estimate

_____

H	T	O
5	1	3
– 1	8	4

d.

Estimate

_____

H	T	O
8	0	7
– 3	1	9

2. Calculate the area of each rectangle. Show your thinking.

FROM 4.3.9

a.

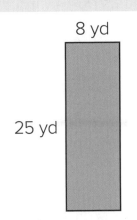

8 yd

25 yd

Area _____ yd²

b.

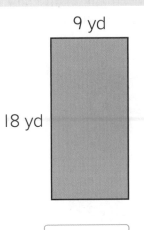

9 yd

18 yd

Area _____ yd²

Each shape is one whole. Color parts to show each fraction.

a. seven-fourths

b. six-fourths

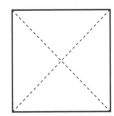

Step In

How could you calculate the perimeter of this field?

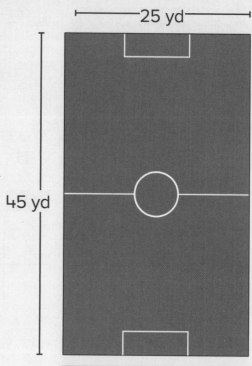

─── 25 yd ───

45 yd

Vincent calculated the perimeter like this.

P = Perimeter

P = (2 × L) + (2 × W)

P = (2 × 45) + (2 × 25)

P = 90 + 50

P = 140 yd

What does **L** and **W** represent?

What steps did he follow?

How many steps did it take him to calculate the perimeter?

Is there a more efficient way to calculate the perimeter?

You could add the length and width first. Then multiply the sum by 2.

P = 2 × (L + W)

P = 2 × (45 + 25)

P = 2 × 70

P = 140 yd

Step Up

1. Complete these to calculate the perimeter of each rectangle.

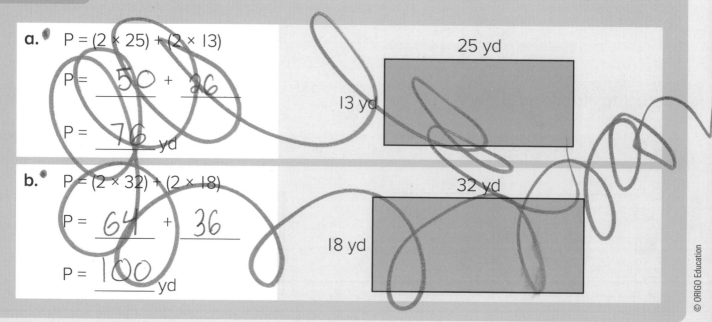

a. P = (2 × 25) + (2 × 13)

P = __50__ + __26__

P = __76__ yd

25 yd

13 yd

b. P = (2 × 32) + (2 × 18)

P = __64__ + __36__

P = __100__ yd

32 yd

18 yd

© ORIGO Education

2. Complete these to calculate the perimeter of each rectangle.

a. ✗

45 yd

30 yd

P = 2 × (45 + 30) ✗

P = 2 × 150 75

P = 300 150 ✗ yd

b. ◆

65 yd

15 yd

P = 2 × (65 + 15)

P = 2 × 80

P = 160 yd

3. Calculate the perimeter of each rectangle. Show your thinking.

a.

27 yd

25 yd

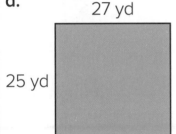

$P = 2 \cdot (l + w)$
$P = 2 \cdot (27 + 25)$
$P = 2 \cdot (52)$
$P = 104$ yd.

Perimeter ___104___ yd

b.

55 yd

52 yd

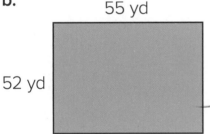

$P = 2 \cdot (l \times w)$
$P = 2 \cdot (55 + 52)$
$P = 2 \cdot (107)$
$P = 214$ yd.

Perimeter ___214___ yd

Step Ahead

Color the ⬤ beside each rule that you could use to calculate the perimeter of a rectangle.

⬤ Add all the distances around the sides.

⬤ Add the length and width. Then multiply the total by 2.

◯ ~~Multiply the length by the width.~~ *Area*

© ORIGO Education

Step In This rectangular backyard has an area of **90 yd²**.

15 yd

What is the length of each unknown side?

How do you know?

The length of the short side is the only length that remains unknown. I will call this length **S**.
S = 90 ÷ 15, or 15 × **S** = 90

Michael has 20 yards of fencing wire.

How much more wire would he need to fence the backyard?

How did you calculate the perimeter of the backyard?

Step Up 1. Measure each side length in centimeters.
Then calculate the perimeter and area.

a.

Perimeter _____ cm

Area _____ cm²

b.

Perimeter _____ cm

Area _____ cm²

c.

Perimeter _____ cm

Area _____ cm²

© ORIGO Education

2. Solve each problem. Show your thinking. Remember to include the units in your answers.

a. A pyramid has a square base. The perimeter of the base is 60 yards. What is the length of each side of the base?

b. Zoe's backyard is a rectangle. The short sides are 5 yards long. The long sides are twice as long. What is the area of her backyard?

c. A room is 10 ft wide and 15 ft long. Another room is 10 ft wide and 18 ft long. What is the difference in area?

d. A rectangular poster has an area of 320 square inches. One longer side is 20 inches. What is the length of one shorter side?

Step Ahead   Solve this problem. Draw a picture to help your thinking.

Oliver buys 150 yards of fencing wire to build a rectangular enclosure. He needs 10 yards of wire left over. Write possible side lengths for the enclosure.

Short side _____ yd

Long side _____ yd

Think and Solve

Clues

- Object D is half the number of grams of Object E.
- Object E is half the number of grams of Object F.
- Object F is 1 kilogram.

Remember, 1 kg = 1,000 g.

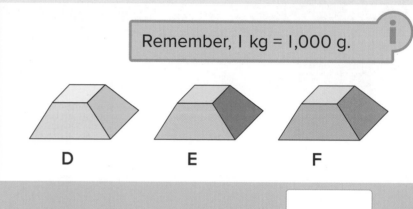

D E F

How many grams is Object D?

Words at Work — Write the answer for each clue in the grid. Use words from the list. Some words are not used.

Clues Across

1. One million is ___ times greater than one hundred thousand.

6. A prime number is any whole number greater than zero that has exactly two ___ factors.

7. You can ___ one factor and halve the other to find different pairs of factors.

8. You multiply length by width to calculate the ___ of a rectangle.

Clues Down

2. A composite number is a whole ___ that has more than two whole number factors.

3. ___ is a factor of 50.

4. 148,601 is ___ than 184,601.

5. You can add length and ___ then double the sum to calculate the perimeter of a rectangle.

| unique |
| five |
| area |
| number |
| perimeter |
| less |
| double |
| two |
| ten |
| more |
| width |

Ongoing Practice

1. For each of these, use the standard subtraction algorithm to calculate the difference between the price and the amount in the wallet.

a.

| $47 | $385 |

H	T	O

b.

| $128 | $263 |

H	T	O

c.

| $116 | $322 |

H	T	O

d.

| $128 | $385 |

H	T	O

FROM 3.6.9

2. Calculate the perimeter of each frame.

a.

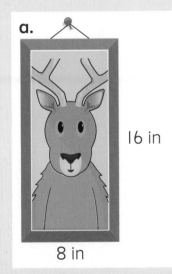

16 in

8 in

2 × 16 = _____

2 × 8 = _____

Perimeter _____ in

b.

6 in

14 in

2 × 6 = _____

2 × 14 = _____

Perimeter _____ in

FROM 4.3.10

Preparing for Module 4

Color the shape and write the fraction to match.

a.

$\frac{3}{4}$

is equivalent to

_____

b.

$\frac{1}{3}$

is equivalent to

_____

Hailey is buying carpet for three rooms in her house. The carpet for each room will be a different color. The main bedroom is 16 feet long and 12 feet wide. The office is 15 feet long and 9 feet wide, and the family room is 23 feet wide by 35 feet long.

At Country Carpets, if you buy less than 250 square feet of the same color carpet, each square foot costs $8. If you buy 250 square feet or more of the same color carpet, the cost for each square foot is $6.

How can Hailey use mathematics to figure out the total cost for carpeting the three rooms? Show your thinking.

 Share another real-world situation where you could use the same thinking.

© ORIGO Education

Which number does not belong?
Show your thinking.

| 9 | 27 | 36 | 17 | 51 |

The number _____ does not belong.

I think this because ...

Share your thinking with another student. They can write their feedback below.

I agree/disagree with your thinking because ...

Feedback from:

 Discuss how the feedback will help you improve the feedback you give.

© ORIGO Education

Step In   Felix is planning a vacation.

This sign shows the flight costs to some locations.

Estimate the **difference** in cost between
a flight to Las Vegas and a flight to Honolulu.

How did you form your estimate?

FLIGHT COSTS

Atlanta	$167
Honolulu	$639
Las Vegas	$198
Palm Springs	$325

$198 is very close to $200, so I
figured out the difference between
$639 and $200. My estimate is $439.

**Estimate the difference in cost between a flight
to Palm Springs and a flight to Atlanta.**

The difference is a little more than $160, because
double $160 is $320. This is only a little less than $325.

What are some other estimates that you can form?

Step Up   1. Estimate the difference in cost between these flights. Show your
thinking by writing the numbers you used to estimate.

a. Pittsburgh $293
Kansas City $155

Estimate $_____

b. Philadelphia $97
Los Angeles $328

Estimate $_____

© ORIGO Education

2. Estimate the difference in cost between these flights. Show your thinking by writing the numbers you used to estimate.

a. Baltimore $252
    Seattle $409

Estimate $_____

b. Madrid $1,205
    Baltimore $252

Estimate $_____

c. Madrid $1,205
    Seattle $409

Estimate $_____

d. Baltimore $252
    London $1,023

Estimate $_____

e. Madrid $1,205
    London $1,023

Estimate $_____

f. London $1,023
    Seattle $409

Estimate $_____

Step Ahead   Write digits in the empty spaces to make two numbers that have a difference of about 500.

a. ☐ ☐ 5 – ☐ 2 6

b. 7 ☐ 3 – ☐ 8 ☐

c. 9 0 ☐ – 3 ☐ ☐

d. 6 5 ☐ – ☐ ☐ 1

Step In

Andre has $245 and buys this guitar. How much money does he have left?

−O C.T.

How do you know?

Alexis used blocks to figure out the amount left over. She started by representing 245.

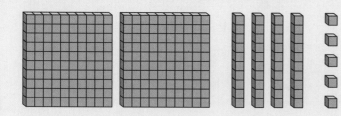

> How can she take away 9 ones when there are only 5 ones blocks?

She then regrouped 1 tens block as 10 ones blocks so there were enough blocks in each place to take away 139.

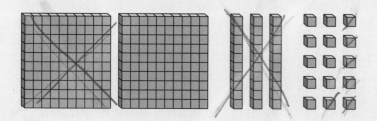

> Does the total value of the blocks change when you regroup?

Cross out blocks to figure out the amount left over.

Follow these steps of the standard subtraction algorithm to calculate the amount left over.

Step 1	Step 2	Step 3	Step 4
Look at the digits in each place. Can you subtract each place easily?	You need 1 ten to help subtract the ones. Cross out the 4 tens and write 3 tens.	Cross out the ones digit and write the new number. 245 is now written as 2 hundreds, 3 tens, and 15 ones.	Subtract the ones. Subtract the tens. Then subtract the hundreds.

Step 1:

X	H	T	O
	2	4	5
−	1	3	9
	1	0	6

Step 2:

X	H	T	O
	2	3 (over 4)	5
−	1	3	9
	1	0	6

Step 3:

X	H	T	O
	2	3 (over 4)	15 (over 5)
−	1	3	9
	1	0	6

Step 4:

	H	T	O
	2	3 (over 4)	15 (over 5)
−	1	3	9
	1	0	6

Step Up

Estimate the difference. Then use the standard subtraction algorithm to calculate the exact difference.

a. Estimate

550

	5	8	7
−		4	5
	5	4	2

b. Estimate

240

	2	8⁸	3¹³
−		5	6
	2	3	7

c. Estimate

220

	4	2	8
−	2	0	7
	2	2	1

d. Estimate

420

	7	4³	2¹²
−	3	1	9
	4	2	3

e. Estimate

620

	6	5	7
−		3	6
	6	2	1

f. Estimate

240

	3²	2¹²	7
−		8	4
	2	4	3

g. Estimate

100

	3	8	5
−	2	8	1
	1	0	4

h. Estimate

380

	8⁷	6¹⁶	5
−	4	8	1
	3	8	4

i. Estimate

250

	5⁴	1¹¹	9
−	2	7	3
	2	4	6

j. Estimate

130

	1	9⁸	1¹¹
−		5	7
	1	3	4

k. Estimate

170

	7⁶	3¹³	6
−	5	6	3
	1	7	3

l. Estimate

200

	4	8⁷	5¹⁵
−	2	7	9
	2	0	6

Step Ahead

Write the missing digits, and regroup if necessary so the answers make sense.

a. ✗

	4	8	2
−	2	7	⊠2
	2	1	0

b. ✓

	3	5⁴	3¹³
−	1	3	8
	2	1	5

c. ✓

	1	7⁶	2¹²
−		4	5
	1	2	7

d. ✓

	5⁴	1¹¹	6
−	1	4	3
	3	7	3

Computation Practice

How do you stop a rhinoceros from charging?

★ Use a ruler to draw a straight line to the correct product. The line will pass through a letter. Write each letter above its matching product at the bottom of the page. Some letters appear more than once.

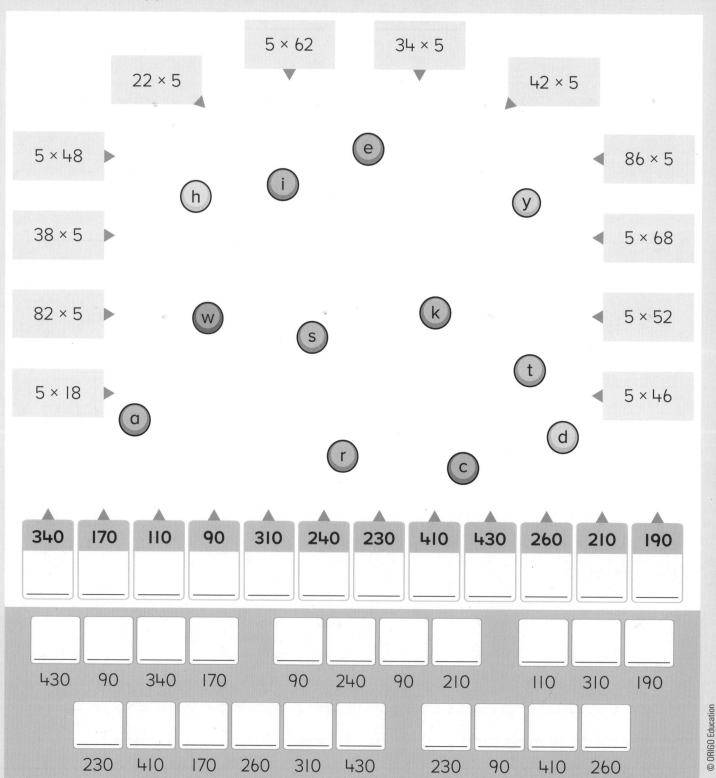

340	170	110	90	310	240	230	410	430	260	210	190
___	___	___	___	___	___	___	___	___	___	___	___

430	90	340	170		90	240	90	210		110	310	190

230	410	170	260	310	430		230	90	410	260

© ORIGO Education

Ongoing Practice

1. Each picture shows one corner of a quadrilateral. Draw the other two sides to make a square or non-square rectangle.

a.
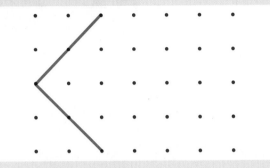

b.
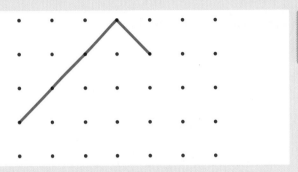

2. Estimate the difference between these prices. Show your thinking by writing the numbers you used to estimate.

a.

$1,319

$297

Estimate $_____

b.

$409

$891

Estimate $_____

c.

$103

$1,279

Estimate $_____

d.

$1,509

$654

Estimate $_____

Preparing for Module 5   Write **10**, **100**, or **1,000** to make each statement true.

a.
10,000 is _____ times greater than 100.

b.
1,000,000 is _____ times greater than 10,000.

c.
100,000 is _____ times greater than 10,000.

d.
1,000,000 is _____ times greater than 1,000.

Step In Imagine you had $345 and you bought this bike. How much money would you have left over?

$78

How do you know?

Follow these steps of the standard subtraction algorithm to calculate the difference.

Step 1	Step 2	Step 3
Look at the digits in each place. Can you subtract each place easily?	You need 1 ten to help subtract the ones. Cross out 4 tens and write 3 tens.	Cross out the ones digit and write the new number. 345 is now written as 3 hundreds, 3 tens, and 15 ones.

Step 1:
```
   H   T   O
   3   4   5
 -     7   8
 _____
```

Step 2:
```
       3
   H   T   O
   3   4̸   5
 -     7   8
 _____
```

Step 3:
```
       3   15
   H   T   O
   3   4̸   5̸
 -     7   8
 _____
```

Step 4	Step 5	Step 6
You need 1 hundred to help subtract the tens. Cross out 3 hundreds and write 2 hundreds.	Add the 10 tens that you have just regrouped to the 3 tens that you already have. You now have 13 tens. Write the number.	345 is now written as 2 hundreds, 13 tens, and 15 ones. Subtract the ones, tens, then hundreds to find the difference.

Step 4:
```
   2   3   15
   H   T   O
   3̸   4̸   5̸
 -     7   8
 _____
```

Step 5:
```
   2   13   15
   H   T    O
   3̸   4̸    5̸
 -      7    8
 _____
```

Step 6:
```
   2   13   15
   H   T    O
   3̸   4̸    5̸
 -      7    8
 _____
   2    6    7
```

Estimate the difference. Then use the standard subtraction algorithm to calculate the exact difference.

a. Estimate

H	T	O
7	9	3
−	7	1

b. Estimate

H	T	O
6	7	8
− 4	7	3

c. Estimate

H	T	O
3	7	7
− 1	0	8

d. Estimate

H	T	O
5	2	8
−	8	1

e. Estimate

H	T	O
4	0	7
− 1	8	2

f. Estimate

H	T	O
5	6	2
−	9	8

g. Estimate

H	T	O
2	3	8
−	5	7

h. Estimate

H	T	O
8	3	7
− 4	5	9

Step Ahead

Draw a picture or write an equation to prove that 4 hundreds, 11 tens, and 15 ones show the same number as 5 hundreds, 2 tens, and 5 ones.

Step In   What does this table show?

How many more people visited the national park in January than in March?

It must be about 11,000 because that is the difference between 17,000 and 6,000.

National Park Visitors	
January	17,475
February	9,305
March	5,950

Ryan used the standard subtraction algorithm to calculate the exact difference.

Look at the letters above the algorithm. What do the letters **TTh** and **Th** mean?

What steps did Ryan follow?

Why did he cross out 4 and write 14?

What does the 14 represent?

TTh	Th	H	T	O
	6	14		
1	7̶	4̶	7	5
−		5	9	5	0
1	1	5	2	5

Step Up   1. Estimate the difference. Then use the standard subtraction algorithm to calculate the exact difference.

a. Estimate

3,100

Th	H	T	O
3	7	1	6
−	6	1	3
3,	1	0	3

b. Estimate

4200

Th	H	T	O
	7	13	
4	8̶	3̶	9
−	6	5	4
4	1	8	5

c. Estimate
18500

TTh	Th	H	T	O
1	13		6	15
2̶	3̶	7	7̶	5̶
−		5	3	1	6
1	8	4	5	9

ORIGO Stepping Stones · Grade 4 · 4.4

Use the information in this table to answer Questions 2 and 3.

National Park Visitors			
	September	October	November
Pine Canyon	7,495	9,030	13,081
Cedar Valley	8,935	13,062	10,306

2. Compare the number of people who visited these national parks. Use the standard subtraction algorithm to calculate the exact difference each month.

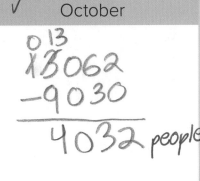

September	October	November
8 9̶3̶5 (8 13) − 7 495 1 440 people	1̶3̶062 (0 13) − 9 030 4 032 people	1̶3̶0̶8̶1̶ (2 10 7 11) − 10,306 2 775 people

3. Use the standard subtraction algorithm to calculate the answers to these.

a. How many more people visited Pine Canyon in November than in October?

1̶3̶081 (0 13)
− 9 030
4 051 people

b. How many fewer people visited Cedar Valley in September than in November?

1̶0̶3̶0̶6̶ (0 9 12 10)
− 8 935
1 371

Step Ahead

Use the standard subtraction algorithm to calculate the answer to this problem.

Pamela's mom wants to buy a new house. She finds one she likes for $327,095. She then sees a similar house for $315,500.

How much money will she save if she buys the less expensive house?

$ 11,595

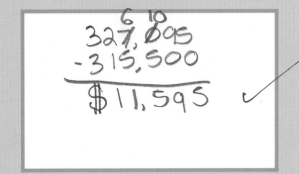

327,095 (6 10)
− 315,500
$11,595

Think and Solve These beans are spread fairly evenly over a grid. Part of the grid has been covered.

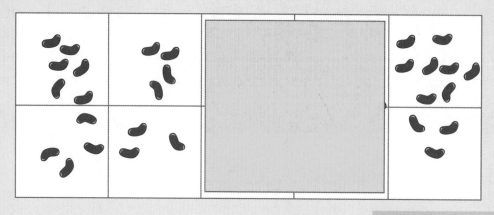

a. Estimate the **total number** of beans on the grid?

About _____ beans

b. Write how you made your estimate.

Words at Work   Write about when you or someone you know needs to estimate a **difference** outside of school. Write at least three sentences to describe your example.

Ongoing Practice

1. Color each rhombus. Use a centimeter ruler to help you decide.

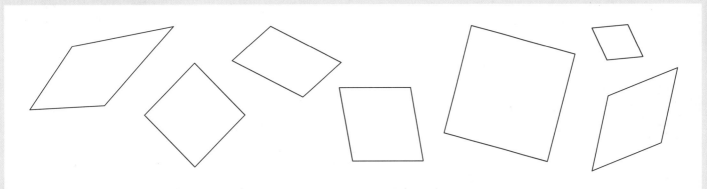

2. Estimate the difference. Then use the standard subtraction algorithm to calculate the exact difference.

a. Estimate

Th	H	T	O
4	8	5	9
− 1	6	4	3

b. Estimate

Th	H	T	O
5	7	2	6
−	5	8	3

c. Estimate

TTh	Th	H	T	O
3	5	8	6	9
−	8	9	4	6

Preparing for Module 5   Solve each problem. Show your thinking.

a. There are 5 stacks of boxes with 6 boxes in each stack. Max has packed 12 bottles into each box. How many bottles did Max pack?

_____ bottles

b. Lomasi bakes 15 trays of muffins for a fair. Each tray holds 16 muffins. How many muffins did she bake?

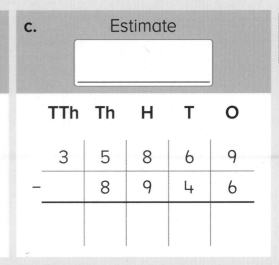

_____ muffins

Step In

Imagine you had $302 and you bought this camera. How much money would you have left over?

$146

How could you figure it out?

I could figure that out in my head by thinking 146 + ? = 302 or 302 - 146 = ?

Victor uses the standard subtraction algorithm to calculate the amount left.

How can he subtract in the ones place when there are no tens to regroup?

H	T	O
3	0	2
− 1	4	6

He decided to regroup the hundreds.

How can he share the hundred between the tens and the ones places?

H	T	O
2		
3̶	0	2
− 1	4	6

What steps does Victor follow to complete the algorithm?

H	T	O
2	9	12
3̶	0̶	2̶
− 1	4	6
1	5	6

He regrouped the hundred as 9 tens and 10 ones.

How could you prove that 2 hundreds, 9 tens, and 12 ones have the same total value as 3 hundreds and 2 ones?

1. Estimate the difference. Then use the standard subtraction algorithm to calculate the exact difference.

a. Estimate

H	T	O
5	0	5
–		7	1

b. Estimate

H	T	O
6	0	3
– 4	7	8

c. Estimate

H	T	O
8	0	4
– 1	5	6

d. Estimate

H	T	O
4	0	7
– 3	2	9

2. Calculate the difference in value. Show your thinking.

a. $503 $730

$ _____

b. $179 $304

$ _____

c. $403 $216

$ _____

d. $608 $419

$ _____

In each diagram, the number in the middle is the difference between the two numbers that are opposite one another. Write numbers in each box so that the diagrams are true.

a.

125

b.

105

Step In   What does this table show?

About how many more people visited the Helpful Hints website than the Gaming Zone website?

Popular Websites	
Site	Visits (monthly)
Helpful Hints	16,035
Toy Shack	8,595
Gaming Zone	12,470

Do you think the difference is greater than or less than 4,000?

How could you calculate the exact difference?

Janice decides to use the standard subtraction algorithm to calculate the exact difference.

What steps should she follow to complete the calculation?

How can she subtract in the tens place when there are no hundreds to regroup?

Complete her calculation to show the difference.

TTh	Th	H	T	O
1	6	0	3	5
− 1	2	4	7	0
				5

Step Up

1. Estimate the difference. Then use the standard subtraction algorithm to calculate the exact difference.

a. Estimate

Th	H	T	O
6	7	0	2
−	5	1	4

b. Estimate

TTh	Th	H	T	O
5	0	3	2	5
−	7	4	1	5

c. Estimate

TTh	Th	H	T	O
3	4	0	6	6
− 1	2	9	9	4

Use the information in this table to answer Questions 2 and 3.

Number of Website Visits			
	March	April	May
Doggy Day Care	11,039	9,503	12,041
Pooch's Paradise	10,257	8,377	14,035

2. Compare the number of website visits each month. Estimate the difference in your head. Then use the standard subtraction algorithm to calculate the exact difference each month.

March	April	May
0 9 13 1X̸Ø3̸9 −10,257 ──── 782	4 9 13 9̸5̸Ø8̸ −8377 ──── 1,126	3 9 13 14̸Ø3̸5 −12041 ──── 1,994

3. Use the standard subtraction algorithm to calculate the answers to these.

a. How many fewer people visited the Doggy Day Care website in April than in May?

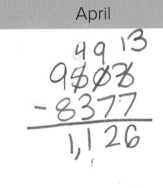

238

b. How many more people visited the Pooch's Paradise website in May than in March?

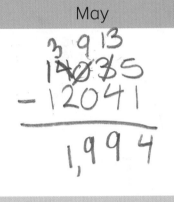

3,778

Step Ahead

The Doggy Day Care site had a total of 201,049 website visits last year. In the previous year it had 145,325 visits. How many more website visits were recorded last year?

1 9 10 10
2̸Ø1̸Ø4̸9
−145325
────
55724

55,724 visits

Computation Practice   How long should an adult giraffe's legs be?

★ Complete the equations. Then write each letter above its matching product at the bottom of the page. Some letters appear more than once.

$4 \times 35 = 140$ **t** $8 \times 65 = 520$ **e**

$6 \times 45 = 270$ **u** $4 \times 55 = 220$ **l**

$6 \times 85 = 510$ **c** $6 \times 35 = 210$ **d**

$4 \times 45 = 180$ **h** $8 \times 55 = 440$ **a**

$8 \times 35 = 280$ **g** $4 \times 65 = 260$ **n**

$6 \times 65 = 390$ **r** $8 \times 45 = 360$ **o**

l	o	n	g		e	n	o	u	g	h
220	360	260	280		520	260	360	270	280	180

t	o		r	e	a	c	h		t	h	e
140	360		390	520	440	510	180		140	180	520

g	r	o	u	n	d
280	390	360	270	260	210

Ongoing Practice

1. Complete each equation. You can use blocks to help. Show your thinking.

a.

$$51 \div 3 = \boxed{}$$

b.

$$68 \div 4 = \boxed{}$$

2. Use the standard subtraction algorithm to calculate the difference.

a.
```
  3 9 6 4 5
- 1 6 3 8 7
_____
```

b.
```
  7 5 2 8 1
- 2 7 1 5 9
_____
```

c.
```
  6 3 0 5 2
- 3 8 0 6 9
_____
```

d.
```
  4 4 6 1 2
- 3 9 5 3 5
_____
```

Preparing for Module 5

Complete the table to show some lengths that you would measure in each unit.

centimeters	meters

Step In   This display shows the prices of some rare baseball cards.

How could you estimate the total cost of the three cards on each shelf?

Choose one card from the top shelf and one card from the middle shelf.

What is the total cost of the two cards?
How did you figure it out?

Choose two cards from the bottom shelf.

What is the difference in cost between these two cards?
How did you figure it out?

$495 $610 $340

$12,325 $14,250 $10,750

$4,050 $2,990 $3,500

Step Up   1. Solve each problem. Show your thinking.

a. Circle one card from each shelf in the Step In. Write the total cost.	b. Imagine you have $5,000. Choose one card that you can buy. Then calculate how much you have left after the purchase.
$_____	$_____

2. Solve each problem. Show your thinking.

a. A club store reported sales of $12,550 for shirts, $6,805 for sweaters, and $2,090 for caps. What were the total sales for shirts and caps?

```
  1  1  1
  12550
   6805
+  2090
 ------
  21,445
```

$ __21,445__

b. A club has 14,225 members who are male and 10,965 members who are female. ~~5,427 members are over 65 years of age.~~ What is the total number of members?

```
   1  1
  14225
+ 10965
 ------
  25,190
```

__25,190__ members

c. A stadium seats 110,000 people. 65,045 tickets were sold on Monday. 27,307 tickets were sold on Tuesday. How many tickets are still available?

```
  1     1
  65045
+ 27307
 ------
  92352
```

```
  0 10 9 9 9 10
  1 1 0 0 0 0
 - 9 2 3 5 2
 ----------
   1 7, 6 4 8
```

__17,648__ tickets

d. A club reported membership sales worth $145,390. This was $27,500 more than the previous year. What were the total sales for the previous year?

```
    3 14 13
  1 4 5 3 9 0
 -   2 7 5 0 0
 -----------
  1 1 7 8 9 0
```

$ __117,890__

Step Ahead

Anoki and Claire put all their cards in a stack. They have a total of 150 cards. Anoki owns 20 more cards than Claire. How many cards does Claire own?

Claire   x
Anoki   x + 20

$x + (20 + x) = 150$

$x + 20 + x = 150$ → 150 -

$2x + 20 = 150$

$2x = 150 - 20$

$2x = 130$

$x = \frac{130}{2} = 65$

__65__ cards

Step In

The large rectangle is one whole. Into how many parts of equal area has it been divided?

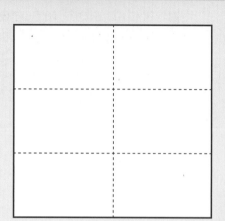

What fraction describes each part?

Shade parts of the rectangle to show four-sixths.

Is four-sixths closer to one whole, one-half, or zero?

Write four-sixths using numerals.

Which digit is the denominator? What does it tell you?
Which digit is the numerator? What does it tell you?

A fraction written in the form $\frac{a}{b}$ is called a **common fraction**.

On this number line, the distance from 0 to 1 is one whole.

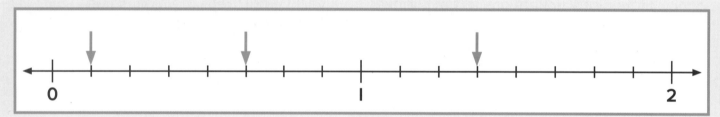

What fractions are the arrows pointing to?
Which is the least fraction? Which is the greatest?

Step Up

1. Each large shape is one whole.
    Shade parts to show each fraction.

a. $\frac{1}{4}$

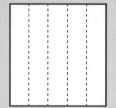

b. $\frac{2}{5}$

c. $\frac{4}{10}$

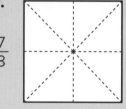

d. $\frac{7}{8}$

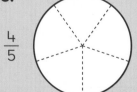

e. $\frac{4}{5}$

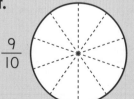

f. $\frac{9}{10}$

g. $\frac{3}{4}$

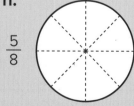

h. $\frac{5}{8}$

ORIGO Stepping Stones · Grade 4 · 4.8

Look at each number line carefully. The distance from 0 to 1 is one whole.
Write the fraction that each arrow is pointing to.

2.

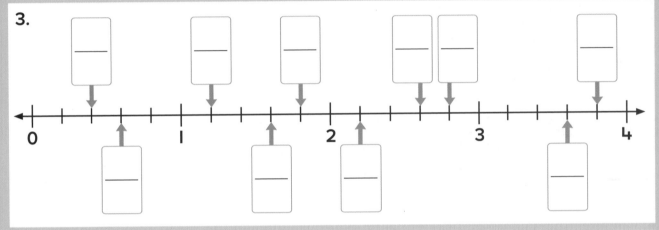

3.

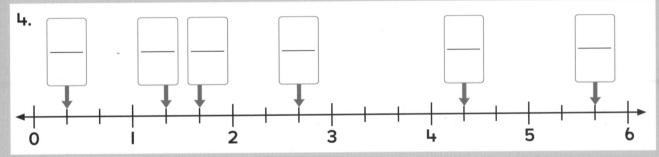

4.

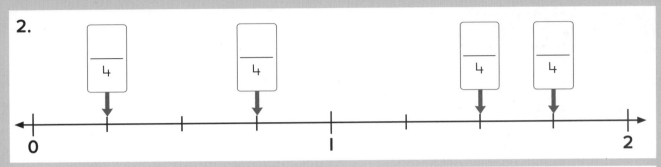

Step Ahead   **a.** Color the star to match these instructions.

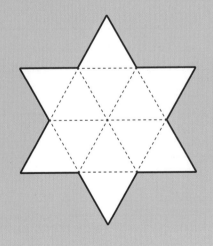

- Color $\frac{1}{3}$ of the star **blue**.

- Color $\frac{1}{4}$ of the star **green**.

- Color the remaining parts **yellow**.

b. What fraction of the star is yellow?

Think and Solve

A unicycle has 1 wheel.

A bicycle has 2 wheels.

A tricycle has 3 wheels.

A car has 4 wheels.

Amos saw 10 vehicles and a total of 37 wheels. Which vehicles did he see?

Words at Work

This algorithm was used to calculate the difference between two numbers.

Write in words how you could figure out the difference another way.

Th	H	T	O
5	16	9	15
6	7	0	5
−	9	5	8
5	7	4	7

© ORIGO Education

1. Solve each problem. Show your thinking.

a. Three friends share the cost of a gift. The gift was $54. How much did each person pay?	**b.** Emilia has 64 yards of fabric. She cuts it into 4 equal pieces. How long is each piece?

$_____

_____ yards

2. Each large shape is one whole. Shade parts to show each fraction.

a. $\frac{5}{8}$  **b.** $\frac{7}{10}$  **c.** $\frac{3}{5}$  **d.** $\frac{1}{4}$

e. $\frac{2}{10}$ 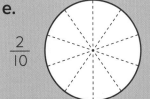 **f.** $\frac{3}{4}$ 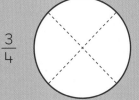 **g.** $\frac{7}{8}$ 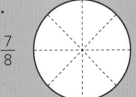 **h.** $\frac{2}{5}$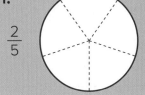

Complete the table to show some capacities that you would measure using each unit.

milliliters	liters

Step In Look at this fraction chart. The top strip is one whole.

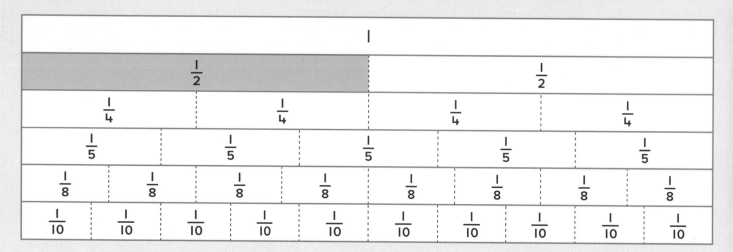

Point to the strip that is divided into two parts. What fraction of that strip is shaded?

What parts of other strips can you shade to show the same fraction? How do you know?

Write the fractions to complete this sentence.

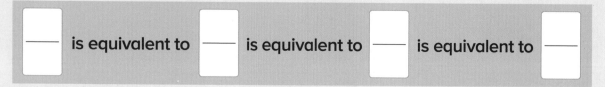

___ is equivalent to ___ is equivalent to ___ is equivalent to ___

What fractions can you show on this number line?

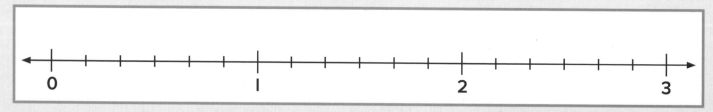

0   1   2   3

How can you tell if two fractions are equivalent on a number line?

What equivalent fractions could you show on this number line?

Step Up 1. Use the fraction chart above to help you write equivalent fractions.

a. $\dfrac{1}{5} = \dfrac{\ }{\ }$

b. $\dfrac{1}{4} = \dfrac{\ }{\ }$

c. $\dfrac{8}{10} = \dfrac{\ }{\ }$

d. $\dfrac{3}{5} = \dfrac{\ }{\ }$

e. $\dfrac{4}{10} = \dfrac{\ }{\ }$

On each number line below, the distance from 0 to 1 is one whole.

2. Write the fractions that the arrows are pointing to.

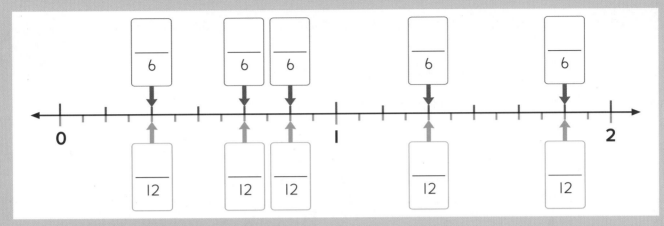

3. Use this number line to help you write equivalent fractions or whole numbers.

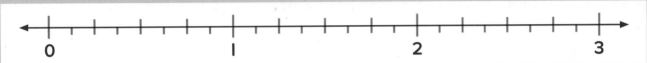

a. $\dfrac{1}{4}$ = ☐

b. $\dfrac{10}{8}$ = ☐

c. $\dfrac{7}{4}$ = ☐

d. $\dfrac{22}{8}$ = ☐

e. $\dfrac{1}{1}$ = ☐

f. $\dfrac{9}{4}$ = ☐

g. $\dfrac{12}{8}$ = ☐

h. $\dfrac{2}{1}$ = ☐

Step Ahead Draw lines to divide the last strip into **sixteenths**. Then complete two different equations involving sixteenths.

$\dfrac{1}{2}$				$\dfrac{1}{2}$			
$\dfrac{1}{4}$		$\dfrac{1}{4}$		$\dfrac{1}{4}$		$\dfrac{1}{4}$	
$\dfrac{1}{8}$	$\dfrac{1}{8}$	$\dfrac{1}{8}$	$\dfrac{1}{8}$	$\dfrac{1}{8}$	$\dfrac{1}{8}$	$\dfrac{1}{8}$	$\dfrac{1}{8}$

a.

b.

Step In   Any whole number can be written as a common fraction.

What are some fractions that are equivalent to 3?

What helps you figure out if they are equivalent?

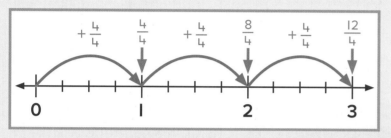

$\frac{4}{4}$ is 1 whole and $\frac{8}{4}$ is 2 wholes so $\frac{12}{4}$ is the same as 3 wholes. You make a jump of $\frac{4}{4}$ between each whole number.

Look at each fraction that is at the same mark as a whole number.

How are the fractions related to the whole numbers?

Each numerator is a multiple of 4.

When I multiply the whole number by the denominator the answer is the same as the numerator.

When I divide the numerator by the denominator the answer is the same as the whole number.

Label each mark on this number line with a common fraction.

Look at the common fractions you wrote at each whole number.

What relationships occur between the numbers?

What is the closest whole number to $\frac{16}{5}$?

How could you figure it out?

I think that identifying which multiple of 5 is closest to 16 will help me figure it out quickly.

© ORIGO Education

1. Write each whole number as a fraction.
Use what you know about multiples to help you.

a.

$1 = \dfrac{\boxed{}}{5}$ $\qquad$ $2 = \dfrac{\boxed{}}{5}$ $\qquad$ $3 = \dfrac{\boxed{}}{5}$ $\qquad$ $4 = \dfrac{\boxed{}}{5}$ $\qquad$ $5 = \dfrac{\boxed{}}{5}$

b.

$1 = \dfrac{\boxed{}}{6}$ $\qquad$ $2 = \dfrac{\boxed{}}{6}$ $\qquad$ $3 = \dfrac{\boxed{}}{6}$ $\qquad$ $4 = \dfrac{\boxed{}}{6}$ $\qquad$ $5 = \dfrac{\boxed{}}{6}$

c.

$1 = \dfrac{\boxed{}}{8}$ $\qquad$ $2 = \dfrac{\boxed{}}{8}$ $\qquad$ $3 = \dfrac{\boxed{}}{8}$ $\qquad$ $4 = \dfrac{\boxed{}}{8}$ $\qquad$ $5 = \dfrac{\boxed{}}{8}$

2. Write each fraction as a whole number.

a. $\dfrac{6}{3} = \boxed{}$ $\qquad$ $\dfrac{21}{3} = \boxed{}$ $\qquad$ $\dfrac{15}{3} = \boxed{}$ $\qquad$ $\dfrac{30}{3} = \boxed{}$ $\qquad$ $\dfrac{24}{3} = \boxed{}$

b. $\dfrac{40}{4} = \boxed{}$ $\qquad$ $\dfrac{20}{4} = \boxed{}$ $\qquad$ $\dfrac{28}{4} = \boxed{}$ $\qquad$ $\dfrac{16}{4} = \boxed{}$ $\qquad$ $\dfrac{36}{4} = \boxed{}$

3. Write the whole number that is closest to each fraction. Show your thinking.

a. $\boxed{}$ is closest to $\dfrac{25}{4}$

b. $\boxed{}$ is closest to $\dfrac{20}{6}$

c. $\boxed{}$ is closest to $\dfrac{37}{5}$

Write each total as a **whole number.** Use what you know about equivalence between whole numbers and fractions to help you.

a. $\dfrac{6}{3} + \dfrac{8}{8} = \boxed{}$

b. $\dfrac{21}{3} + \dfrac{10}{5} = \boxed{}$

c. $\dfrac{40}{4} + \dfrac{42}{6} = \boxed{}$

Computation Practice   How many birds can you put in an empty cage?

★ Complete the equations. Then write each letter above its matching answer at the bottom of the page.

190 + 470 = 660 **e**	540 − 260 = 280 **e**	810 − 560 = 250 **f**
380 + 590 = 970 **t**	160 + 380 = 540 **s**	450 − 190 = 260 **y**
520 − 370 = 150 **h**	280 + 370 = 650 **p**	460 + 280 = 740 **a**
370 + 450 = 820 **i**	560 − 380 = 180 **t**	350 − 180 = 170 **t**
250 + 670 = 920 **m**	480 + 350 = 830 **r**	940 − 180 = 760 **o**
860 − 670 = 190 **t**	920 − 630 = 290 **o**	570 + 360 = 930 **t**
570 + 280 = 850 **t**	820 − 550 = 270 **n**	930 − 350 = 580 **n**
350 + 290 = 640 **a**	450 + 360 = 810 **e**	

o n e , a f t e r t h a t
760 270 280 640 250 970 660 830 930 150 740 850

i t ' s   n o t   e m p t y
820 190 540   580 290 180   810 920 650 170 260

Ongoing Practice

1. Write the number of minutes past the hour and the number of minutes to the next hour. Then write the time on the digital clock.

a.

[ ] minutes past [ ]

[ ] minutes to [ ]

b.

[ ] minutes past [ ]

[ ] minutes to [ ]

2. Use the number line to help you write equivalent fractions or whole numbers.

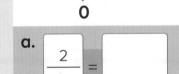

0   1   2   3

a. $\frac{2}{4}$ = [ ]

b. $\frac{3}{4}$ = [ ]

c. $\frac{5}{4}$ = [ ]

d. $\frac{24}{8}$ = [ ]

e. $\frac{1}{1}$ = [ ]

f. $\frac{10}{4}$ = [ ]

g. $\frac{12}{8}$ = [ ]

h. $\frac{3}{1}$ = [ ]

Preparing for Module 5

Complete the table to show some masses you would measure using each unit.

grams	kilograms

Step In   Tyler and Dallas share five licorice sticks.

If they share the sticks equally, how much will each person have?

They will need to break one of the sticks to share it. Then they will have two whole pieces each, plus half a piece each.

Imagine all the licorice sticks were broken in half before sharing. How would you write each share as a common fraction?

A **mixed number** is a whole number and a common fraction added together, and written as a single number without the addition symbol.

$2 + \frac{1}{2}$ ➞ $2\frac{1}{2}$

Will each person still have the same amount as before? How do you know?

Mixed numbers can be made by joining amounts in different ways.

$3\frac{2}{5}$ is equivalent to $3 + \frac{1}{5} + \frac{1}{5}$

$3\frac{2}{5}$ is equivalent to $2 + 1 + \frac{2}{5}$

How could you show $4\frac{3}{8}$ as the sum of other numbers?

Step Up   1. Read each problem, and look at the picture. Write the total as a mixed number.

a. Daniel bought two sandwiches. The shaded parts show how much he ate. How much did Daniel eat?

Daniel ate [ ] sandwiches.

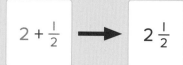

b. Beatrice's family bought three pizzas. The shaded parts show how much they ate. How much did they eat?

They ate [ ] pizzas.

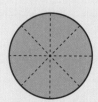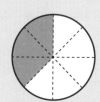

2. Each large shape is one whole. Shade the shapes to show the mixed number.

a.
$3\frac{1}{5}$

b.
$2\frac{3}{6}$

c.
$1\frac{5}{8}$

d.
$3\frac{2}{4}$

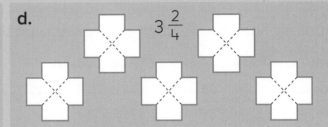

3. Each large shape is one whole. Complete each equation to show how much is shaded. Write the total as a **common fraction**, then as a **mixed number**.

a.

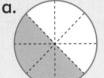

$$\frac{}{} + \frac{}{} + \frac{}{} = \frac{}{} = \boxed{}$$

b.

$$\frac{}{} + \frac{}{} + \frac{}{} = \frac{}{} = \boxed{}$$

c.

$$\frac{}{} + \frac{}{} + \frac{}{} = \frac{}{} = \boxed{}$$

d.

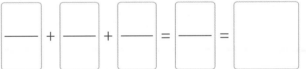

$$\frac{}{} + \frac{}{} + \frac{}{} = \frac{}{} = \boxed{}$$

Step Ahead

Write three different ways to make a total of $3\frac{6}{8}$. You can draw pictures to help.

$\boxed{} = 3\frac{6}{8}$ $\boxed{} = 3\frac{6}{8}$ $\boxed{} = 3\frac{6}{8}$

Step In   Ashley says this picture shows $2\frac{4}{6}$.

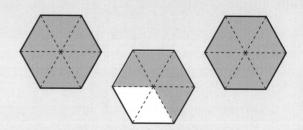

Gabriel says it shows $\frac{16}{6}$.

Who is correct? Why?

A number line can be used to show the position of both amounts.

What do you notice about their position?

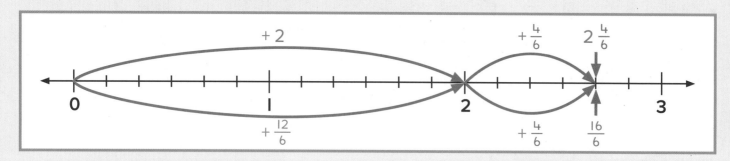

Use red to circle the mark for $\frac{8}{6}$.

What is the equivalent mixed number?

How do you know?

Use green to circle the mark for $1\frac{5}{6}$.

What is the equivalent common fraction?

> Mixed numbers and common fractions are two different ways of representing the same amount. Could you use mixed numbers to describe amounts less than 1? Why or why not?

Step Up   1. Write the equivalent mixed number and common fraction that describe the parts that are shaded. Each large shape is one whole.

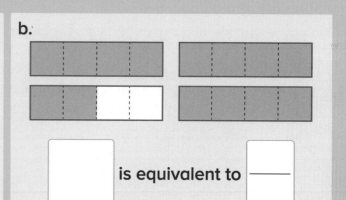

a.

[   ] is equivalent to ⎯⎯⎯

b.

[   ] is equivalent to ⎯⎯⎯

2. Complete the common fractions and mixed numbers.

a.

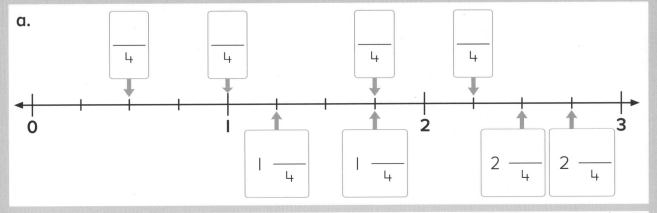

b.

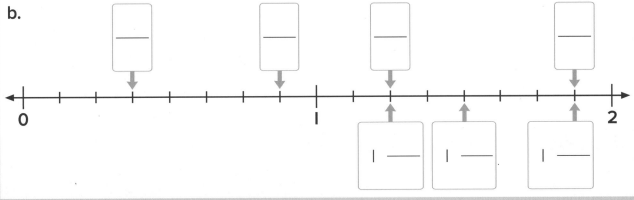

3. Use the number line in Question 2b to write these mixed numbers as common fractions.

a. $1\dfrac{10}{8} = \dfrac{}{}$ b. $1\dfrac{14}{8} = \dfrac{}{}$ c. $1\dfrac{9}{8} = \dfrac{}{}$ d. $1\dfrac{12}{8} = \dfrac{}{}$ e. $1\dfrac{16}{8} = \dfrac{}{}$

4. Write **<**, **>**, or **=** to complete each number sentence.
Use the number line in Question 2b to help you.

a. $\dfrac{8}{8}$ ◯ $1\dfrac{1}{8}$ b. $\dfrac{11}{8}$ ◯ $1\dfrac{3}{8}$ c. $1\dfrac{7}{8}$ ◯ $1\dfrac{2}{8}$ d $1\dfrac{10}{8}$ ◯ $\dfrac{16}{8}$

Step Ahead   Circle the greater fraction. Show your thinking. $1\dfrac{2}{5}$ or $\dfrac{16}{10}$

Think and Solve These equations have no operation symbols.

Use three different symbols to make these totals.
Each total must be a **whole number**.

greatest possible total	$5 \bigcirc 5 \bigcirc 5 \bigcirc 5 = \boxed{}$
least possible total	$5 \bigcirc 5 \bigcirc 5 \bigcirc 5 = \boxed{}$

Words at Work   Color the boxes for the words that make true sentences.

a. $1\frac{7}{8}$ is | **greater** | **less** | than $\frac{13}{8}$.

b. $\frac{14}{5}$ is | **greater** | **less** | than $2\frac{1}{5}$.

c. One-half is | **equivalent to** | **not equivalent to** | to three-sixths.

d. In a common fraction, the digit on the | **top** | **bottom** | is the

numerator, and the denominator is the digit on the | **top** | **bottom** |.

e. A | **whole** | **mixed** | number is a | **whole** | **mixed** |

number and a common fraction added together.

f. Mixed numbers | **are** | **are not** | used to describe amounts

less than one whole.

Developing the practices ▶

Ongoing Practice

1. Write the number of minutes. Draw jumps on the number line to show your thinking.

a. 36 min + 45 min

[ ] _____ minutes

b. 65 min − 27 min

[ ] _____ minutes

FROM 3.2.9

2. Each large shape is one whole. Shade the shapes to show the mixed number.

a. $1\frac{2}{3}$

b. $1\frac{4}{6}$

c. $2\frac{1}{4}$

d. $3\frac{5}{8}$

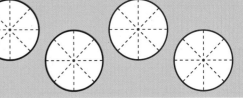

FROM 4.4.11

Preparing for Module 5   Solve each problem. Show your thinking.

a. Shiro packed 3 cans into one box. 2 cans weighed 300 g. The third can weighed 200 g. What is the total mass of the 3 cans?

_____ g

b. Grace's drink bottle holds one liter of water. At recess she drinks $\frac{1}{4}$ of the water. How much water is left in the bottle?

___ L

© ORIGO Education

Each player in an online design competition builds their dream house. The player who receives the greatest number of likes wins. The table shows the number of likes one week before the competition closes.

At the end of the competition, Sara has 15,000 more likes and Andre's score doubles. Marcos and Mana each have 5,000 more votes.

Player	Likes
Marcos	11,109
Sara	5,113
Mana	11,187
Andre	10,079

Who has won the competition and by how many points? Show your thinking.

How did you decide which strategies to use?

Richard says there are at least three fractions between $\frac{10}{12}$ and $\frac{11}{6}$. Katherine does not agree.

Do you agree or disagree with Richard? Show your thinking.

I agree/disagree with Richard because ...

Share your thinking with another student. They can write their feedback below.

I agree/disagree with your thinking because ...

Feedback from:

Discuss how the feedback helps you see the same problem from a different point of view.

© ORIGO Education

Step In   Compare the number of counters in these two bags.
What do you notice?

There are three **times as many** counters in Bag B as Bag A.

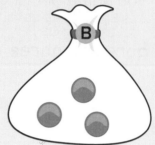

Draw more counters to show 5 times as many counters in Bag B.

How could you compare the length of these two strips?

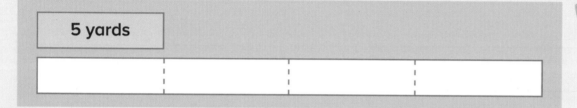

5 yards

How long is the longer strip?

How do you know?

I will call the short strip **S**. I can figure out the length of the long strip by calculating 4 × **S**.

Step Up   1. Draw counters in the empty bag to match the statement.

a.

Bag B has 4 times as many counters as Bag A.

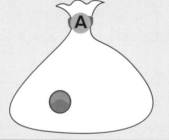

b.

Bag C has 5 times as many counters as Bag D.

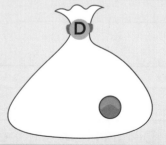

2. Color the long strip to match each label.

a.

| 7 yards | | | | | | 4 times as long |

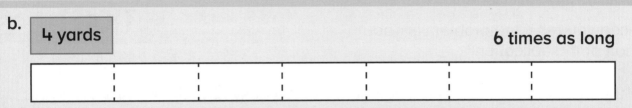

b.

| 4 yards | | | | | | 6 times as long |

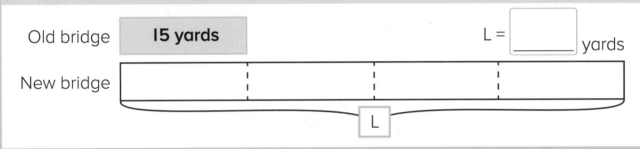

3. Write numbers in the diagram to solve the problem. Then write the answer.

a. The old bridge was 15 yards long. The new bridge will be 4 times as long. What will be the length of the new bridge?

Old bridge | 15 yards

L = _____ yards

New bridge

L

b. Aston has $25 in savings. Camila has 5 times as much. How much does Camila have in savings?

Aston

S = $_____

Camila

S

Step Ahead   Draw a diagram to help solve this problem. Then write the answer.

Kevin's grandparents live 25 miles away. The distance to his aunt's house is 3 times farther. How far away is his aunt's house?

_____ miles

Step In

Fiona sells 45 raffle tickets for a school fundraiser.
Owen sells three more tickets than Fiona.

RAFFLE TICKET

How many raffle tickets has Owen sold?

How can you tell if the problem is about addition or multiplication?

Write the numbers that can help you figure out the answer in the diagram below.

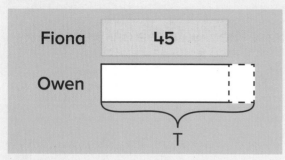

| Fiona | 45 |
| Owen | |

T

I will call the number of tickets Owen sold T.
T = 45 + 3

Class 4B sold three times as many raffle tickets as Fiona.

Complete this diagram to calculate the number of raffle tickets Class 4B sold.

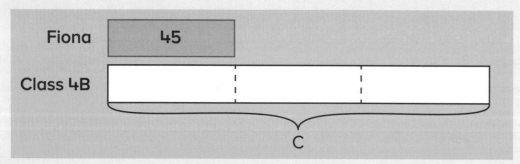

| Fiona | 45 |
| Class 4B | |

C

What is different about the two diagrams?

Step Up

1. Write **multiplication** or **addition** to show how you would solve each problem. You do not need to solve the problem.

a. A plane ticket costs $245. It costs $35 more to reserve the seat. What is the total cost?

_____

b. An economy-class ticket costs $96. A ticket in first class costs 5 times as much. What is the cost of a first-class ticket?

_____

2. Complete the tape diagrams to solve each problem.
Then write an equation to match.

a. The first game was watched by 2,075 supporters. 150 more supporters
watched the second game. What was the attendance at the second game?

First game	2,075	

Second game		150

b. Cathy sold 789 copies of her book last month. She sold 420 copies this month.
She has 45 copies left to sell. How many books has she sold?

Last month	789	

This month		

c. It takes 30 seconds to reheat a pie. If the pie is frozen it takes 6 times as long.
How many seconds does it take to heat a frozen pie?

Reheating	30	

From frozen						

Step Ahead Draw a diagram to help solve this problem. Then write the answer.

A coach orders uniforms for some of team players. Shirts cost $16 each and
shorts cost $10 each. What is the total cost of 5 uniforms?

$ _____

Computation Practice

★ Write each total in the grid below.

Across	Down
a. 18 + 345	**a.** 333 + 28
c. 255 + 28	**b.** 328 + 29
e. 537 + 19	**c.** 49 + 216
f. 28 + 119	**d.** 336 + 38
h. 525 + 29	**g.** 38 + 427
j. 19 + 635	**i.** 527 + 48
l. 423 + 29	**j.** 59 + 612
n. 19 + 547	**k.** 18 + 438
o. 157 + 39	**l.** 434 + 28
p. 217 + 48	**m.** 19 + 256

Ongoing Practice

1. Calculate the part in parentheses and write the new problem. Then complete the equation.

a. $25 + (6 \times 5)$

$\boxed{25} + \boxed{30} = \boxed{55}$

b. $(30 + 6) \div 4$

$\boxed{} \div \boxed{} = \boxed{}$

c. $(7 - 4) \times 8$

$\boxed{} \times \boxed{} = \boxed{}$

d. $30 - (30 \div 10)$

$\boxed{} - \boxed{} = \boxed{}$

e. $18 + (16 \div 2)$

$\boxed{} + \boxed{} = \boxed{}$

f. $200 + (3 \times 7)$

$\boxed{} + \boxed{} = \boxed{}$

2. Complete the diagram to solve the problem. Then write an equation to match.

a. Emily has saved $15 to buy a guitar. The guitar costs four times as much as she has saved. What is the price of the guitar?

Savings | $15

Cost of guitar | ☐

b. Hugo has $75. Allan has $4 more than Hugo. How much money does Allan have?

Hugo | $75

Allan | ☐

Preparing for Module 6

Write the product for each part. Then write the total.

a.

$5 \times 10 = \boxed{}$ $5 \times 4 = \boxed{}$

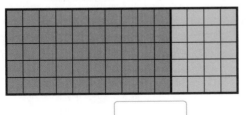

$5 \times 14 = \boxed{}$

b.

$3 \times 10 = \boxed{}$ $3 \times 4 = \boxed{}$

$3 \times 14 = \boxed{}$

Step In

Cary has 35 pencils. He has seven times as many pencils as his sister Charlotte.

How many pencils does Charlotte have?

How does this diagram match the word problem?

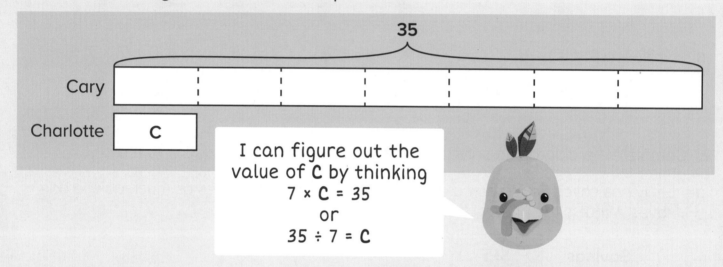

I can figure out the value of **C** by thinking
$7 × C = 35$
or
$35 ÷ 7 = C$

Complete these two equations to show the answer.

$7 × \boxed{} = 35$ $35 ÷ 7 = \boxed{}$

Step Up

1. Solve each problem. Complete the diagram to show your thinking.

a. Awan is 75 years old. He is 3 times as old as Jennifer. What is Jennifer's age?

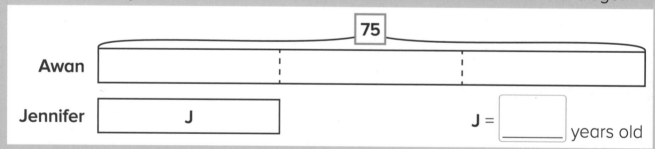

$J = \boxed{}$ years old

b. 5 tickets cost \$100. What is the cost of one ticket?

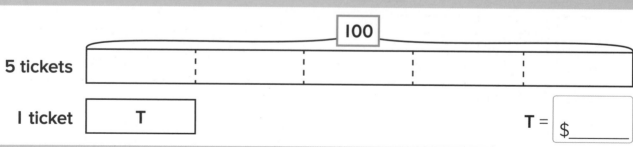

$T = \$\underline{}$

© ORIGO Education

2. Draw a diagram to solve each problem. Then write the answer.

a. Ethan has 60 stamps in his collection. He has 4 times as many stamps as Carmen. How many stamps does Carmen have?

_____ stamps

b. Grade 4 raised $45 in cake sales. They raised 3 times as much as Grade 2. What amount did Grade 2 raise?

$_____

c. The cost of a gift is equally shared by 4 friends. The price of the gift is $120. What amount will each friend pay?

$_____

Step Ahead Solve this problem. Draw diagrams or write equations to show your thinking.

Jacinta buys 5 bags of soil and 4 bags of fertilizer. It costs $40 to buy the soil and another $40 to buy the fertilizer. The next day she buys 2 more bags of soil and one more bag of fertilizer. What amount does she pay on the second day?

$_____

Step In   This picture shows the mass of Michelle's bag.

Harvey's bag weighs 3 lb less than Michelle's.

How does this diagram match the problem?

45 lb

Michelle's bag	
Harvey's bag	? 3

What is the mass of Harvey's bag? How do you know?

Look at this diagram. How would you describe the relationship of Juan's bag to Michelle's bag?

45 lb

Michelle's bag		
Juan's bag	?	

What thinking would you use to figure out the mass of Juan's bag?

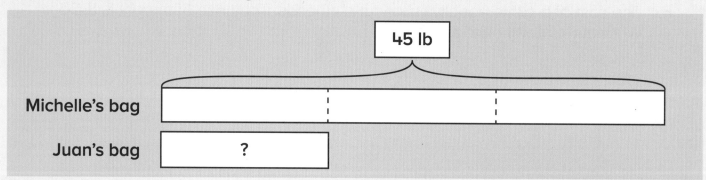

I would think multiplication.
3 × ? = 45

Step Up   1. Write **division** or **subtraction** to show how you would solve each problem. You do not need to solve the problem.

a. A tie costs half as much as a shirt. The shirt costs $52. What is the cost of the tie?

_____

b. A jacket costs $90. A sweater costs $15 less. What is the cost of the sweater?

_____

2. Complete the tape diagrams to solve each problem. Then write equations to match.

a. Nam scores 96 points. He scores twice as many points as his brother. How many points does his brother score?

Nam	96 points

Brother

_____

b. A tiger weighs 385 lb. A lion weighs 90 lb less. How much does the lion weigh?

Tiger	385 lb

Lion

_____

c. Kayla has $1,045 in her savings account. She buys a new couch and has $650 left. What is the cost of the couch?

Savings	$1,045

Couch

_____

d. Corey earned $150 in one month. He earned three times as much as his sister. How much did his sister earn?

Corey	$150

Sister

_____

Step Ahead

Two friends spent $40 in total at the movies. The tickets cost three times as much as the snacks.

How much did the tickets cost?

$_____

Think and Solve Look at this sorting diagram.

Factors of 24	2	Factors of 32

Write each of these numbers in the correct part of the diagram.

4   12   3   16   1   6   8

Write three other numbers that do **not** belong in any part of the diagram.

☐ ☐ ☐

Words at Work   Look at this diagram. Write a word problem to match. Then write how you calculated the answer.

15

Ongoing Practice

1. Write an equation to match each problem. Then calculate the answer.

a. Blake has $20. He buys lunch for $12, then shares the change equally between his two children. How much did they each receive?

$_____

b. Kylie has $50. She buys 3 tickets for $8 each. How much money does she have left?

$_____

2. Solve each problem. You can draw diagrams to help your thinking.

a. Kevin buys 2 concert tickets for $45 each. Eva buys 2 tickets to the same concert. She uses a coupon and saves $15 off each ticket. How much did she pay?

$_____

b. Peter is 12 years old. His dad is four times as old as Peter. His grandma is 30 years older than the combined ages of Peter and his dad. How old is Peter's grandma?

_____

Preparing for Module 6

Solve each problem. Show your thinking.

a. There are 4 fish tanks. Each tank has 12 goldfish and 12 black fish. How many fish are there in total?

_____ fish

b. The coach bought 4 bats for $15 each and 4 balls for $11 each. How much was spent in total?

$_____

Step In

This is a photo of Brady and his family. He is 8 years old. Brady has been circled.

Read the clues and figure out the age of each person in the photo.

CLUE 1	My dad is 10 times as old as my little brother.
CLUE 2	I am twice as old as my little brother.
CLUE 3	My dad is 4 years older than my mom.
CLUE 4	My mom is 4 times older than my sister.
CLUE 5	My grandpa is 5 years older than the combined age of my mom and dad.

How old is each person in the photo?

In what order did you use the clues?

Think about the ages of the people in your family. What clues could you write?

Step Up

Solve each problem. Draw diagrams to help your thinking.

a. A concert hall seats 2,450 people. 1,890 tickets have been sold. How many more tickets are available?

_____ tickets

b. Lulu cycles 12 miles each day. Kyle cycles 15 miles each day. How much farther does Kyle cycle after 5 days?

_____ miles

c. Four friends share the cost of a gift. They each pay $36. How much did the gift cost?

$_____

d. It costs $54 to buy 6 yards of chain. What is the cost of buying 5 yards of the same chain?

$_____

Step Ahead

Brianna spent $26 on drinks for a party. The food cost 5 times as much as the drinks.

How much did she spend on food and drinks in total?

Show your thinking.

$_____

ORIGO Stepping Stones · Grade 4 · 5.5

171

Step In

José has to cut paper streamers for a party.
Each streamer has to be about 70 centimeters long.

The whole roll is 4 meters long.

Will there be enough on the roll for 10 streamers?
How do you know?

In the word **centimeter**, **centi** means one-hundredth. A related word is **cent**, because one cent is one-hundredth of a dollar.

I know that 100 centimeters is equivalent to 1 meter. So how many centimeters is equivalent to 4 meters? What is the total length of 10 streamers at 70 centimeters each?

This picture shows the length of Carol's arm span in centimeters.

How could you **say** the length of Carol's arm span?

How could you **write** the length of Carol's arm span?

_____ meter _____ centimeters

You could also abbreviate the units.

Step Up

I. Write each distance using centimeters.

a. 5 m = _____ cm

b. 50 m = _____ cm

c. 13 m = _____ cm

d. 130 m = _____ cm

e. 280 m = _____ cm

f. 4,300 m = _____ cm

2. Write the missing lengths in meters and centimeters. Then draw lines to show where the other lengths are located on the measuring tape.

| 0 m 87 cm | ____ m ____ cm | 1 m 34 cm |

90 cm 100 cm 110 cm 120 cm 130 cm 140 cm

| 1 m 90 cm | ____ m ____ cm | 2 m 27 cm | ____ m ____ cm |

190 cm 200 cm 210 cm 220 cm 230 cm 240 cm

| ____ m ____ cm | 3 m 18 cm | ____ m ____ cm | 3 m 35 cm |

290 cm 300 cm 310 cm 320 cm 330 cm 340 cm

| 4 m 0 cm | ____ m ____ cm | 4 m 39 cm | ____ m ____ cm |

400 cm 410 cm 420 cm 430 cm 440 cm 450 cm

Step Ahead   Write the lengths of these dinosaur babies in centimeters.

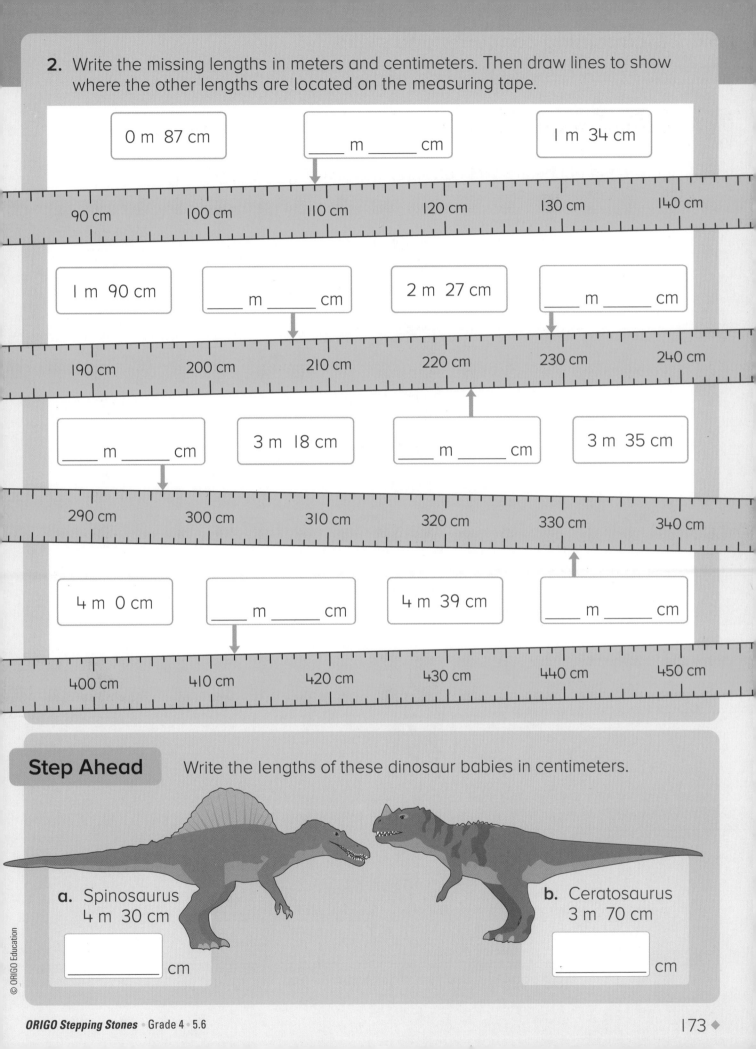

a. Spinosaurus
4 m 30 cm

_____ cm

b. Ceratosaurus
3 m 70 cm

_____ cm

Computation Practice   What are macaroni, gentoo, chinstrap, and emperor?

★ Complete the equations. Write each letter above its matching product at the bottom of the page.

$2 \times 74 =$ _____   e $5 \times 65 =$ _____   u

$8 \times 58 =$ _____   o $4 \times 46 =$ _____   t

$5 \times 42 =$ _____   n $2 \times 28 =$ _____   s

$4 \times 38 =$ _____   f $8 \times 63 =$ _____   p

$2 \times 16 =$ _____   n $5 \times 57 =$ _____   s

$8 \times 36 =$ _____   e $4 \times 74 =$ _____   i

$5 \times 26 =$ _____   y $5 \times 16 =$ _____   g

$4 \times 27 =$ _____   p

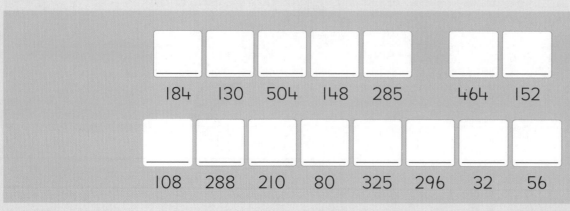

184	130	504	148	285		464	152

108	288	210	80	325	296	32	56

Ongoing Practice   I. Calculate the area of each rectangle. Show your thinking.

a.

6 yd

12 yd

Area _____ yd²

b.

18 yd

2 yd

Area _____ yd²

2. Write the missing lengths in meters and centimeters. Then draw lines to show where the other lengths are located on the measuring tape.

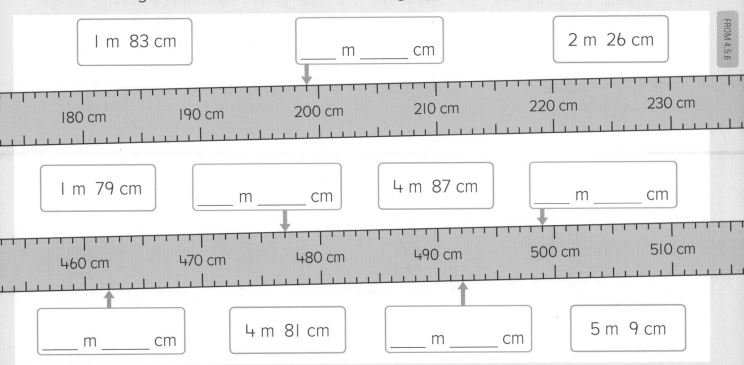

1 m 83 cm

_____ m _____ cm

2 m 26 cm

180 cm   190 cm   200 cm   210 cm   220 cm   230 cm

1 m 79 cm

_____ m _____ cm

4 m 87 cm

_____ m _____ cm

460 cm   470 cm   480 cm   490 cm   500 cm   510 cm

_____ m _____ cm

4 m 81 cm

_____ m _____ cm

5 m 9 cm

Preparing for Module 6   Solve each problem. Show your thinking.

a. The green hose is 5 feet longer than the red hose. The red hose is 11 feet long. How long is the green hose?

_____ ft

b. Emma joins 2 ribbons. One ribbon is 7 inches long. The total length is 13 inches. How long is the other ribbon?

_____ in

5.7 Length: Introducing millimeters

Step In

Some types of ants are shorter than one centimeter.

One millimeter is one-tenth of the length of a centimeter.

How many millimeters are equivalent to one centimeter?
How many millimeters are equivalent to five centimeters?

How long is each ant from head to tail? How do you know?

> A short way to write **millimeter** is **mm**.

Step Up

1. List things in your classroom that are a **little less** than one millimeter thick and a little **more than** one millimeter thick.

A little less than one millimeter thick	A little more than one millimeter thick

2. Measure and label the dimensions of these stickers in millimeters.

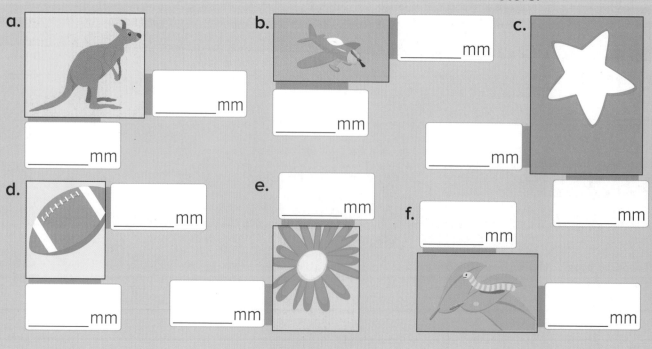

a. _____mm   _____mm

b. _____mm   _____mm

c. _____mm   _____mm

d. _____mm   _____mm

e. _____mm   _____mm

f. _____mm   _____mm

3. Complete these.

a.

I centimeter is equivalent to _____ millimeters.

b.

100 centimeters is equivalent to _____ millimeters.

c.

I meter is equivalent to _____ millimeters.

4. Use the information in Question 3 to help you complete these.

a.

40 centimeters is equivalent to _____ millimeters.

b.

85 centimeters is equivalent to _____ millimeters.

5. Write these lengths in millimeters.

a.

5 cm 4 mm = _____ mm

b.

13 cm 8 mm = _____ mm

Step Ahead

Complete the machine's missing numbers.

Centimeters (cm)   Millimeters (mm)

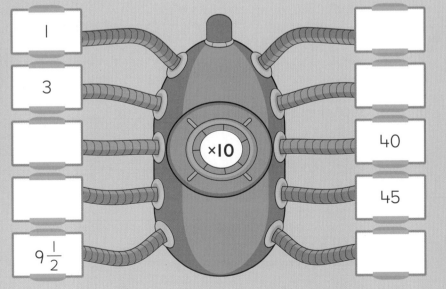

Step In

This block measures 10 cm.

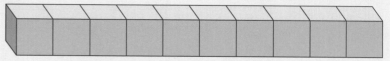

How many millimeters are equivalent to 10 cm? How do you know?

How many centimeters are equivalent to one meter? How can you check?

You could check by placing 10 tens blocks along one side of a meter stick.

In the word **millimeter**, **milli** means one-thousandth. A related word is **millipede**, a creature with so many legs it was once thought they have about 1,000.

How many millimeters equal one meter? How did you figure it out?

A **decimeter (dm)** is a metric unit of length that is not used often but it helps to show an important pattern.

Look at this diagram.
What pattern do you see?

How many centimeters are equivalent to one decimeter?

How many decimeters are equivalent to one meter?

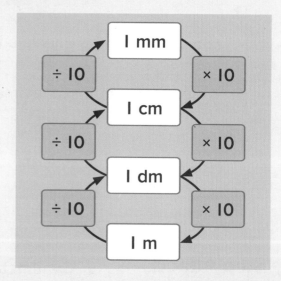

Step Up

1. Write the metric unit of length you would use with measuring each of these.

   a. length of a pencil

   b. length of a paper clip

   c. length of a car

   d. thickness of a ruler

2. Complete each of these.

a.
6 meters
is equivalent to

_____ mm

b.
9 meters
is equivalent to

_____ mm

c.
4 meters
is equivalent to

_____ mm

d.
11 meters
is equivalent to

_____ mm

e.
15 meters
is equivalent to

_____ mm

f.
$7\frac{1}{2}$ meters
is equivalent to

_____ mm

3. Complete this table to show equivalent lengths.

Millimeters (mm)	Centimeters (cm)	Meters (m)
	100	1
		$2\frac{1}{2}$
4,500		

4. Solve each problem. Show your thinking.

a. The sides of a triangle measure 64 mm, 3 cm, and 7 cm. What is the total length of the two longer sides?

_____ mm

b. The sides of a triangle measure 76 mm, 8 cm, and 10 cm. What is the difference between the lengths of the two shorter sides?

_____ mm

Step Ahead Write these measurements in order from **least** to **greatest**.

8 m	700 cm	9,000 mm	40 cm	500 mm

Think and Solve A 2 m × 2 m garden has 8 m of fencing wire and 8 fence posts. Each post is 1 m apart.

A 3 m × 3 m garden is being built the same way.

a. The new garden will need [   ] fence posts.

b. The new garden will need [   ] m of fencing wire.

I m {

Words at Work Imagine a friend was away from school when you were learning about how meters, centimeters, and millimeters are related. Write how you would explain the relationship to them.

© ORIGO Education

Ongoing Practice

1. Write possible dimensions for each rectangle.

a.

_____ yd

_____ yd

Area is 48 yd²

b.

_____ yd

_____ yd

Area is 90 yd²

c.

_____ yd

_____ yd

Area is 27 yd²

d.

_____ yd

_____ yd

Area is 56 yd²

2. **a.** Measure and write the dimensions of this sticker in millimeters. Then complete the statements below.

_____ mm

_____ mm

b. _____ millimeters is equivalent to 3 centimeters.

c. _____ millimeters is equivalent to 30 centimeters.

d. _____ millimeters is equivalent to 100 centimeters.

Preparing for Module 6

Write **feet**, **inches**, or **yards** to show how you would measure each of these.

a. window _____

b. adult's height _____

c. large playground _____

d. child's shoe _____

e. door _____

f. swimming pool _____

FROM 4.3.9

FROM 4.5.7

© ORIGO Education

ORIGO Stepping Stones · Grade 4 · 5.8

181 ◆

Step In Where have you heard of kilometers before?

Rapid City
II miles
18 km

I have seen kilometers as **km** on some road signs.

Some people participate in a 5-kilometer fun run every year.

5-km FUN RUN

Kilometers are used to measure long distances.

How is "kilo" different from "milli"?

Look at a meter stick.

How many meter sticks would you need to make one kilometer?

> ⓘ In the word **kilometer**, kilo means one thousand. A related word is **kilogram**, which is equal to 1,000 grams. A short way to write kilometer is km.

What do you remember about the decimeter?

Some other metric units of length are not used often but help show the relationship between metric units of length.

> ⓘ A **dekameter** is equal to 10 meters. A short way to write dekameter is dam. A **hectometer** is equal to 100 meters. A short way to write hectometer is hm.

Look at this diagram.

What pattern do you see?

How is the relationship between kilometers and meters the same as the relationship between meters and millimeters?

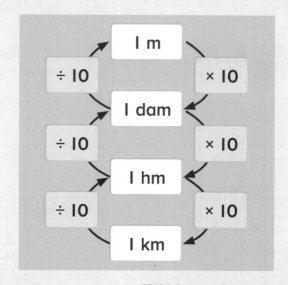

Step Up

1. Complete these.

a. 1 kilometer is equivalent to

_____ m

b. 10 kilometers is equivalent to

_____ m

c. 100 kilometers is equivalent to

_____ m

2. a. These hiking trails are in Yellowstone National Park. Circle the trails that are between 1,000 and 6,000 meters long. Use the information above to help you.

Duck Lake $1\frac{6}{10}$ km

Howard Eaton $11\frac{3}{10}$ km

Mystic Falls 4 km

Ice Lake $\frac{5}{10}$ km

Rescue Creek $12\frac{8}{10}$ km

Garnett Hill $11\frac{8}{10}$ km

Pelican Valley $10\frac{8}{10}$ km

Lava Creek $5\frac{6}{10}$ km

Beaver Ponds 8 km

Two Ribbons 2 km

b. Jack's family hiked about 15,000 m. Which trails might they have walked? Write two different combinations.

_____

_____

3. Write these lengths in meters.

a.

16 km 8 m = _____ m

b.

5 km 40 m = _____ m

Step Ahead

Complete the table below to show equivalent distances.

mm	cm	dm	m	dam	hm	km
			600			$\frac{6}{10}$

Step In

Look at this balance picture. Each small box has the same mass.

How could you figure out the mass of each one?

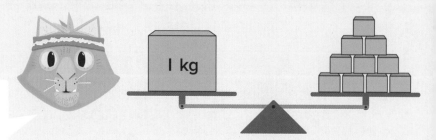

I know that 1,000 grams is equivalent to 1 kilogram.

Look at this scale.

How could you write the mass shown?

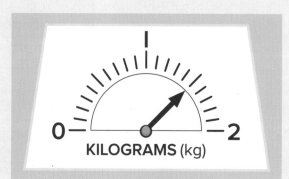

I would write $1\frac{5}{10}$ kg or $1\frac{1}{2}$ kg.

How could you write the equivalent mass in grams?

Complete these statements.

$1\frac{1}{2}$ kg is equivalent to _____ g

$\frac{1}{10}$ kg is equivalent to _____ g

What are some other kilogram masses that you can say in grams?

Step Up

1. Read the scales carefully. Write each mass in grams.

a.
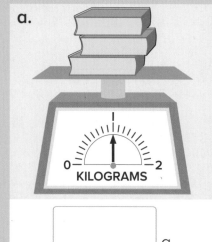

_____ g

b.
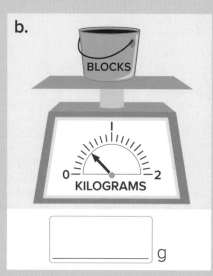

BLOCKS

_____ g

c.
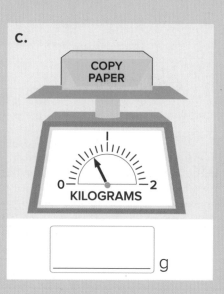

COPY PAPER

_____ g

2. Read the scales carefully. Write each mass in grams.

a.

_____ g

b.

_____ g

c.

_____ g

3. Write the equivalent mass in grams.

a. 4 kilograms

is equivalent to

_____ g

b. 9 kilograms

is equivalent to

_____ g

c. $2\frac{1}{2}$ kilograms

is equivalent to

_____ g

d. $3\frac{7}{10}$ kilograms

is equivalent to

_____ g

e. $6\frac{1}{10}$ kilograms

is equivalent to

_____ g

f. $4\frac{9}{10}$ kilograms

is equivalent to

_____ g

Step Ahead

Write the equivalent mass in grams. Use the number line to help your thinking.

$1\frac{1}{4}$ kg _____ g

$1\frac{3}{4}$ kg _____ g

$5\frac{1}{4}$ kg _____ g

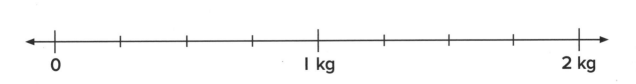

Computation Practice   Did you hear about the girl who does tap dancing?

★ For each division card, use a ruler to draw a straight line to a multiplication card that could help you figure out the quotient. The line will pass through a number and a letter. Write each letter above its matching number at the bottom of the page. Some multiplication cards are used more than once.

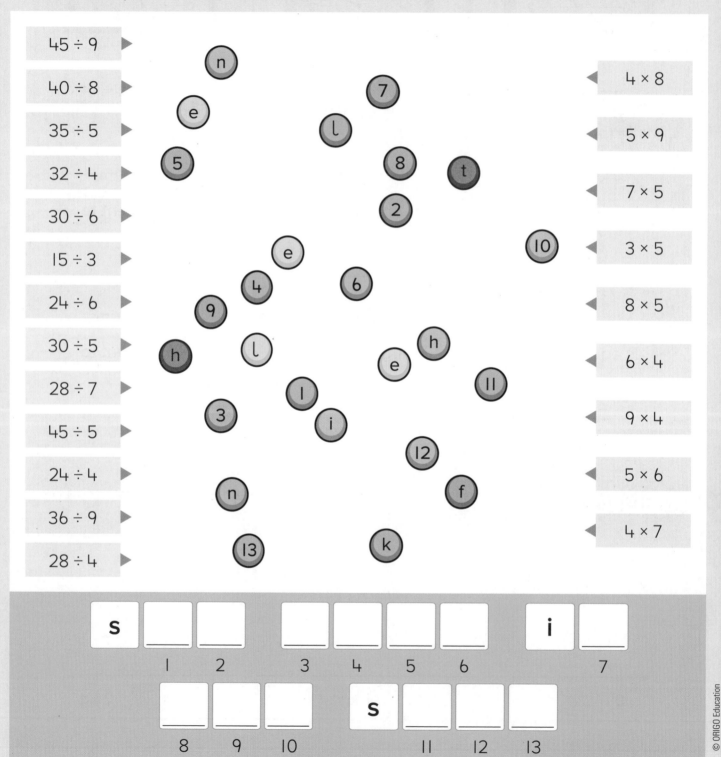

Ongoing Practice

1. Complete the calculation to figure out the perimeter of each rectangle.

a. P = 2 × (33 + 17)

P = 2 × ▢

P = ▢ yd

33 yd

17 yd

b. P = 2 × (28 + 16)

P = 2 × ▢

P = ▢ yd

28 yd

16 yd

2. Write the missing numbers in this table to show equivalent lengths.

Centimeters (cm)	Meters (m)	Kilometers (km)
	1,000	
	100	
		$\frac{1}{2}$
	250	

Preparing for Module 6

Fold a square of paper in half, and in half again to make a quarter-turn tester. Use the tester to measure each corner of this shape.

a. Color the corner red if it fits the tester corner exactly.

b. Color the corner blue if it is larger than the tester corner.

c. Color the corner green if it is smaller than the tester corner.

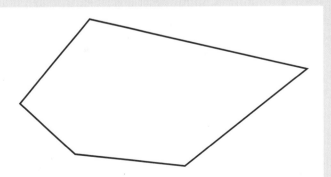

© ORIGO Education

ORIGO Stepping Stones · Grade 4 · 5.10

187 ◆

Step In   What amount of juice is in this pitcher?

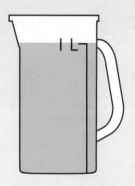

Imagine the juice was poured equally into two containers.
How many milliliters would be in each container?

> I know there are 1,000 mL in
> 1 liter. 500 mL is half of 1,000 mL.

Imagine the juice was poured equally into ten containers.
How many milliliters would be in each container?
How do you know?

This container holds more than one liter.
How much juice is in the container?

Complete these statements.

$1\frac{1}{2}$ L is equivalent to [   ] mL $\frac{1}{10}$ L is equivalent to [   ] mL

What are some other liter amounts that you can say in milliliters?

Step Up   1. Look carefully at the scale on each container.
Then write the amount of water in each.

a.

[   ] mL

b.

[   ] mL

c.
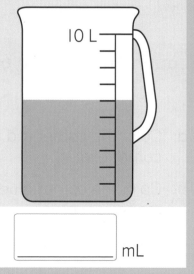
[   ] mL

2. Look carefully at the scale. Then write the amount in each container.

a.

_____ mL

b.

_____ mL

c.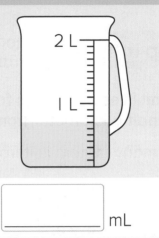

_____ mL

3. Write the equivalent capacity in milliliters.

a.
8 liters

(is equivalent to)

_____ mL

b.
2 liters

(is equivalent to)

_____ mL

c.
$4\frac{1}{2}$ liters

(is equivalent to)

_____ mL

d.
$2\frac{8}{10}$ liters

(is equivalent to)

_____ mL

e.
$5\frac{4}{10}$ liters

(is equivalent to)

_____ mL

f.
$3\frac{7}{10}$ liters

(is equivalent to)

_____ mL

Step Ahead

Write the amount of liquid in the container.
Then explain in words how you figured it out.

_____ mL

Step In

Two friends live at opposite ends of the same straight street.
They arrange to meet at a store on their street.

Abigail lives 34 meters from the store and Isaac
lives half a kilometer from the store.

How many meters is it from Abigail's home to Isaac's home?

Complete this table to help you calculate the answer.

Kilometers	Meters
$\frac{1}{4}$	
1	1,000
10	

I cm = 10 mm
I m = 100 cm
I m = 1,000 mm
I kg = 1,000 g
I L = 1,000 mL

Step Up

1. Solve each problem. Show your thinking and be sure to use the correct units in your answer.

a. Ribbon A is 500 mm long. Ribbon B is taped to the end of Ribbon A, so the total length is 63 cm. How long is Ribbon B?

_____ mm

b. Before an operation, a dog weighs $3\frac{4}{10}$ kg. Afterward, it is $3\frac{1}{10}$ kg. How many grams has the dog lost?

_____ g

c. Naomi rides 450 meters to Cole's house. Together they ride 3 km to the mall. How many meters does Naomi ride in total to the mall?

_____ m

d. A pitcher holds $1\frac{1}{2}$ liters of water. Luis pours out some water and there is now 900 mL of water left. How much water was poured out?

_____ mL

2. Solve each problem. Show your thinking.

a. There are 3 alligators. The smallest is $1\frac{1}{4}$ meters long. The second is 68 cm longer than the smallest one. The largest is 2 meters 10 cm longer than the second one. How long is the largest alligator?

_____ cm

b. Carrina needs 1 kg of dried fruit for a baking fundraiser. She has 5 packets that each weigh 125 g. How much more dried fruit does she need?

_____ g

c. A 2-meter long piece of lumber is being cut for shelves. Each shelf will be 645 mm long, and there are two shelves. How much lumber will be left after the shelves are cut?

_____ mm

d. 4 small bottles of water are poured into a 2 L pitcher. Each small bottle holds 300 mL of water. How many more whole bottles of water can be poured into the pitcher?

_____ bottles

Step Ahead   Complete each equation. Check your answers.

a. 10 cm + _____ cm = 170 mm

b. _____ km + 540 m = 10,540 m

c. 3,000 cm + _____ m = 3,200 cm

d. _____ mm + 3 m = 4,863 mm

Think and Solve

a. The product of three numbers is 140. Two of the numbers are 2 and 10.

What is the third number? _____

b. Write numbers to show two different equations.

$5 \times \boxed{} \times \boxed{} = 120$ $5 \times \boxed{} \times \boxed{} = 120$

Words at Work   Write words from the list to complete true sentences.

a. A _____ is 1,000 times as long as one meter.

b. A _____ is 100 times longer than one centimeter.

c. A _____ is 1,000 times heavier than one gram.

d. A _____ is 1,000 times more than one milliliter.

| mass |
| kilogram |
| liter |
| capacity |
| kilometer |
| meter |
| length |

e. Kilograms and grams are units of _____.

f. Centimeters and millimeters are units of _____.

g. Liters and milliliters are units of _____.

© ORIGO Education

Ongoing Practice   **1.** Solve each problem. Show your thinking.

a. A rectangular garden is 3 times as long as it is wide. The garden is 4 yards wide. What is the area of the garden?

[_____] yd²

b. A square corral is 1,600 square yards in area. The corral is 40 yards long. What is the perimeter of the corral?

[_____] yards

FROM 4.3.12

2. Look carefully at the scale. Write the amount of juice in each pitcher.

a.

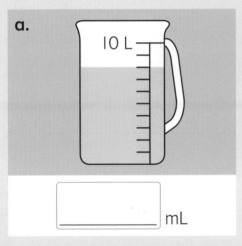

[_____] mL

b.

[_____] mL

c.

[_____] mL

FROM 4.5.11

Preparing for Module 6

a. Use green to color the corners that match a green pattern block corner.

b. Use orange to color the corners that match an orange pattern block corner.

c. Use yellow to color the corners that match a yellow pattern block corner.

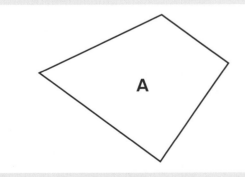

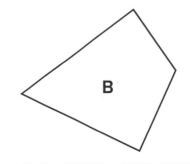

 Gemma is packing books into boxes. The contents of each box must weigh 12 kg. Book A weighs 2 kg, book B weighs $\frac{1}{2}$ kg, and book C weighs 750 grams.

a. How many of the lightest books can be packed into one box?

b. How many of the heaviest books can be packed into one box?

c. If books that are different in mass are packed into one box, how many different combinations can be packed?

Show your thinking.

 Share another real-world situation where you could use the same thinking.

ORIGO Stepping Stones · Grade 4 · Module 5

© ORIGO Education

Samuel has written the following clues about his blended family. He says the only way to figure it out is to start with clue 3.

Clues

1. Mr. Arnott is three times as old as his son Alex.

2. Mrs. Arnott is six years younger than Mr. Arnott.

3. Jacob is 9 years old.

4. Thomas is one-fifth of Mrs. Arnott age.

5. Caitlyn and Chloe are twins who are five years older than Jacob.

6. Mr. Arnott is double the age of Josh, who is double the age of Jacob.

Do you agree or disagree with Samuel? Show your thinking.

I agree/disagree with Samuel because ...

Share your thinking with another student. They can write their feedback below.

I agree/disagree with your thinking because ...

Feedback from:

Discuss how you can apply this feedback to a different problem.

Step In Donna is painting the ceiling of a room.

She needs to know the area of the ceiling
to calculate how much paint to buy.
The dimensions are shown on the right.

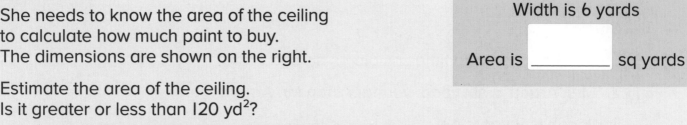

Length is 24 yards

Width is 6 yards

Area is _____ sq yards

Estimate the area of the ceiling.
Is it greater or less than 120 yd²?
How could you calculate the exact area?

Wendell drew this grid to help. He split 24 into tens and ones
then multipled 6 × 20 and 6 × 4.

6

20   4

You can split a rectangle
into parts to find the
partial products.

How could you use this strategy to calculate 5 × 36?

Step Up 1. Write the dimensions around the grid. Color the tens part blue
and the ones part yellow. Write the product for each part then
add the products to calculate the area of the grid.

a.   4 × 17

4 × __10__ = _____

4 × __7__ = _____

Area _____ sq units

b.
                      5 × 23

5 × _____ = _____

5 × _____ = _____

Area _____ sq units

2. Color the tens part red and the ones part blue. Then write each product. Add the two partial products and write the total.

a.

3 × 47

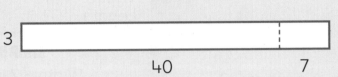

3   40   7

3 × _____ = _____

3 × _____ = _____

Total _____

b.

7 × 58

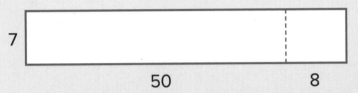

7   50   8

7 × _____ = _____

7 × _____ = _____

Total _____

c.

3 × 64

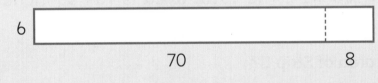

3   60   4

3 × _____ = _____

3 × _____ = _____

Total _____

d.

6 × 78

6   70   8

6 × _____ = _____

6 × _____ = _____

Total _____

Step Ahead

A handyman is working on a garden path. The path is 7 bricks wide and 35 bricks long. He has 200 bricks. How many more bricks does he need to order? Show your thinking.

_____ bricks

Step In   Compare these dimensions of two paper strips.

© ORIGO Education

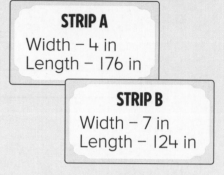

STRIP A
Width – 4 in
Length – 176 in

STRIP B
Width – 7 in
Length – 124 in

Which strip has the greater area?
How do you know?

How could you calculate the exact area of each strip?

Look at this diagram.

| 4 | 400 | 280 | 24 |
| | 100 | 70 | 6 |

How has the rectangle been split?

What does each of the red numbers represent?

How could you use the diagram to calculate
the total area of Strip A?

> You can split a rectangle
> into parts to find the
> **partial products**.

I would add the areas of the smaller rectangles.
That is 400 + 280 + 24. The total area is 704 sq inches.

How could you calculate the exact area of Strip B?

Step Up   I. Calculate each partial product. Then add the partial products and
        write the total.

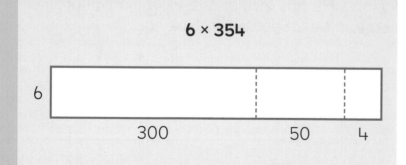

6 × 354

| 6 | | | |
| | 300 | 50 | 4 |

6 × _____ = _____

6 × _____ = _____

6 × _____ = _____

Total _____

2. Write the dimensions around the rectangle. Calculate each partial product.
Then add the partial products and write the total.

a.

4 × 289

_____ × _____ = _____

_____ × _____ = _____

_____ × _____ = _____

Total _____

b.

7 × 534

_____ × _____ = _____

_____ × _____ = _____

_____ × _____ = _____

Total _____

c.

6 × 391

_____ × _____ = _____

_____ × _____ = _____

_____ × _____ = _____

Total _____

Step Ahead

Split the rectangle to show 7 × 307.
Then write equations to calculate the area.

Total _____

Computation Practice

What can an elephant have that no other animals can have?

★ Complete the equations. Find each answer in the grid below and cross out the letter above. Then write the remaining letters at the bottom of the page.

860 – 310 = _____

420 + 220 = _____

680 – 470 = _____

520 + 260 = _____

780 – 610 = _____

340 + 230 = _____

750 – 410 = _____

320 + 160 = _____

570 – 250 = _____

120 + 470 = _____

670 – 450 = _____

310 + 460 = _____

550 – 240 = _____

280 + 610 = _____

770 – 520 = _____

430 + 220 = _____

660 – 420 = _____

440 + 350 = _____

980 – 360 = _____

B	L	O	N	G	E	A	R
150	780	890	550	790	320	760	250
S	B	G	R	E	Y	B	E
220	580	240	770	480	470	210	560
L	E	P	T	R	U	N	K
230	180	330	640	650	310	620	340
H	A	N	D	T	U	S	K
490	630	260	170	660	590	460	570

Write the letters in order from the ❋ to the bottom-right corner.

© ORIGO Education

Ongoing Practice

1. Write the equivalent capacity in milliliters.

FROM 4.5.11

a.
2 liters

is equivalent to

_____ mL

b.
5 ½ liters

is equivalent to

_____ mL

c.
2 4/10 liters

is equivalent to

_____ mL

d.
8 liters

is equivalent to

_____ mL

e.
3 7/10 liters

is equivalent to

_____ mL

f.
3 ½ liters

is equivalent to

_____ mL

2. Color the tens part red and the ones part blue. Then write each product.
Add the two partial products and write the total.

FROM 4.6.1

a.
3 × 36

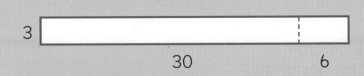

3 × _____ = _____

3 × _____ = _____

Total _____

b.
6 × 47

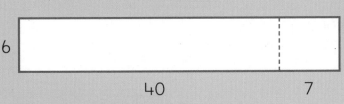

6 × _____ = _____

6 × _____ = _____

Total _____

Preparing for Module 7

Complete each equation. Show your thinking.

a.
Half of 150 is [_____]

b.
Half of 240 is [_____]

Step In

Luke is planning a summer vacation for his family. He buys three package deals to the Grand Canyon.

GRAND CANYON

VACATION PACKAGES
$1,849

Estimate the total amount he will pay.

Do you think it will be more or less than $5,000?

How could you calculate the exact cost?

Isabelle drew this diagram to help her thinking.

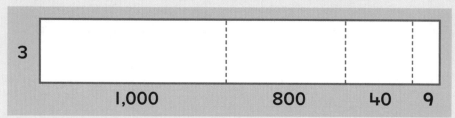

3

1,000   800   40   9

How did she split the rectangle?

Complete the equations to show each partial product. Then add the partial products to find the total.

Compare the parts of the rectangle in the diagram to each partial product. Color the part of the rectangle that shows 3 × 800.

$3 \times 1,000 =$ _____

$3 \times 800 =$ _____

$3 \times 40 =$ _____

$3 \times 9 =$ _____

Total _____

Step Up

1. Calculate each partial product.
Then write the total of the four products.

4 × 2,125

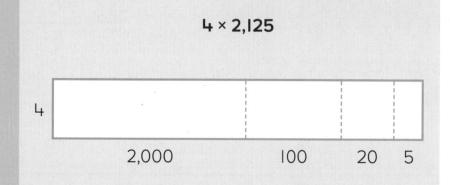

4

2,000   100   20   5

$4 \times 2,000 =$ _____

$4 \times 100 =$ _____

$4 \times 20 =$ _____

$4 \times 5 =$ _____

Total _____

2. Label the dimensions for each part and write equations to calculate each partial product. Then add the partial products and write the total.

a.

3 × 2,178

_____

×_____ = _____

×_____ = _____

×_____ = _____

×_____ = _____

Total _____

b.

4 × 1,795

_____

×_____ = _____

×_____ = _____

×_____ = _____

×_____ = _____

Total _____

c.

2 × 3,208

_____

×_____ = _____

×_____ = _____

×_____ = _____

Total _____

Step Ahead

Use yellow to color the part of the rectangle that shows 8 × 20.
Use blue to color the part of the rectangle that shows 8 × 500.
Use red to color the part of the rectangle that shows 8 × 3,000.

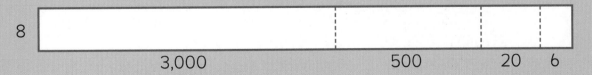

8   3,000   500   20   6

Step In

New turf is being laid in a playground. This diagram shows the dimensions of the playground.

Estimate the amount of turf needed.

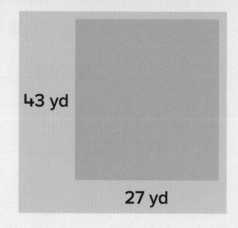

43 yd

27 yd

I know 40 × 3 is 120.
40 × 30 is ten times more, so about 1,200 sq yards of turf will be needed.

How could you calculate the exact amount of turf to order?

Giselle drew this diagram.
What does her diagram show?

How did she split the rectangle?

What does each red number represent?

What is the unknown value? How do you know?

How could you calculate the total area of the playground?

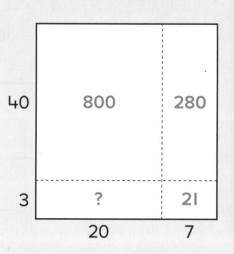

	800	280
40	800	280
3	?	21
	20	7

Step Up

1. Calculate each partial product.
Then write the total of the four products.

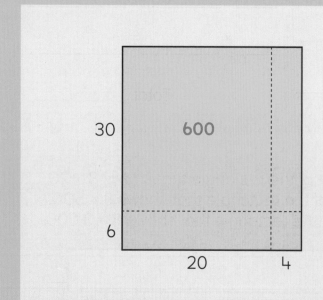

36 × 24

30 × _____ = _____

30 × _____ = _____

6 × _____ = _____

6 × _____ = _____

Total _____

2. Write an equation to calculate each partial product.
Then write the total of the four products.

a.

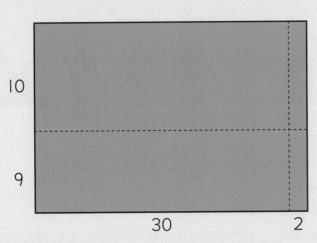

19 × 32

_____ × _____ = _____

_____ × _____ = _____

_____ × _____ = _____

_____ × _____ = _____

Total _____

b.

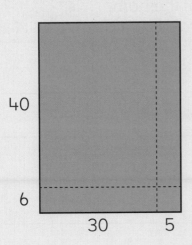

46 × 35

_____ × _____ = _____

_____ × _____ = _____

_____ × _____ = _____

_____ × _____ = _____

Total _____

Step Ahead   Calculate each product. Show your thinking.

a.
17 × 45 = [ ]

b.
38 × 27 = [ ]

Think and Solve

Which two shaded shapes have the same area?

_____

A   B   C

Words at Work

Write in words how you would solve this problem.
There are many possible answers.

A new rectangular barn is being built on a ranch. It needs space for 5 stables that are each at least 15 feet by 15 feet in area. It also needs a single storage and work area of 275 square feet. What could be the dimensions of the barn?
Draw and label a diagram to show how the stables and storage space fit in your barn.

1. Solve each problem. Show your thinking.

a. A bottle holds 2 liters of water. Some water is poured out. There is $\frac{1}{2}$ liter left. How much water was poured out?

_____ mL

b. Logan pours 600 mL of fruit juice and 900 mL of water into a pitcher. How much liquid is in the pitcher?

L

FROM 4.5.12

2. Label the dimensions for each part and write equations to calculate each partial product. Then add the partial products and write the total.

FROM 4.6.3

a. 4 × 3,065

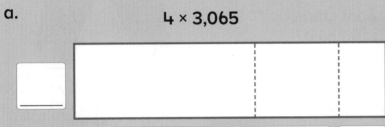

_____ × _____ = _____

_____ × _____ = _____

_____ × _____ = _____

Total _____

b. 3 × 2,504

_____ × _____ = _____

_____ × _____ = _____

_____ × _____ = _____

Total _____

Preparing for Module 7

Use a halving strategy to complete this diagram.

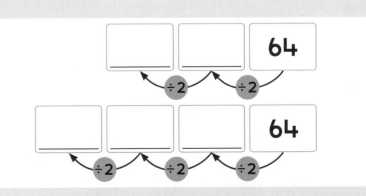

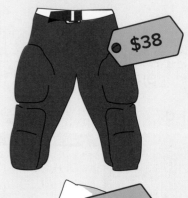

Step In   The Bay City Tigers need to buy 25 pairs of shorts.

How could you calculate the total cost of the shorts?

Dena wrote the partial products to calculate the total.

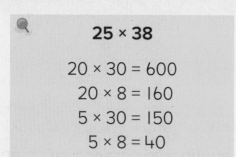

25 × 38

$20 \times 30 = 600$
$20 \times 8 = 160$
$5 \times 30 = 150$
$5 \times 8 = 40$

What is the total cost of the shorts? How do you know?

The Mountain Warriors need to buy 12 team shirts and 12 pairs of shorts. What will be the total cost?

I will call the total cost of the shirts and shorts T.
$T = (45 + 38) \times 12$

Step Up   1. The Cincinnati Chargers need to buy eight complete uniforms. Use the uniform prices above. What is the total cost?

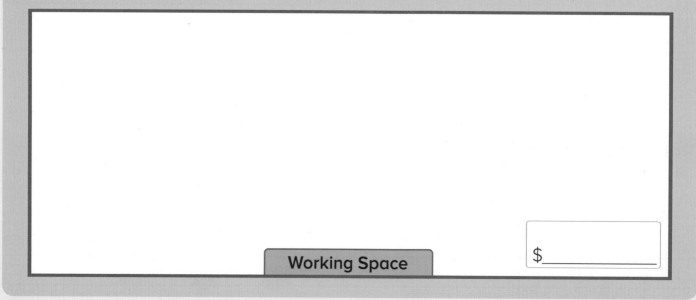

Working Space

$ _____

2. Solve each problem. Show your thinking.

a. Sweaters cost $47 each. This is $15 more than a cap. 25 caps were sold at one game. What is the total sales of caps?

$ _____

b. A stadium parking lot has 38 rows. Each row has 42 spaces. 200 spaces are reserved for staff. How many spaces are for supporters?

_____ spaces

c. Team A season tickets cost $1,407 and Team B season tickets cost $45 less. Richard buys 5 Team B season tickets. What does he pay?

$ _____

d. A team of 18 players bought boots for $36 and socks for $9. What was the total cost for the team?

$ _____

Step Ahead   Write a word problem to match this equation. Then calculate the product.

$42 \times 13 = $ _____

Step In A zoo keeper compares the length of two young alligators.

The first alligator is 2 feet long. The second alligator is 21 inches. Which alligator is longer? How do you know?

> There are 12 inches in 1 foot.

Complete this table.

Feet	1	2	3	5	10	15	20
Inches	12						

How did you calculate the number of inches in 10, 15, and 20 feet?

The largest young alligator in the zoo is $2\frac{1}{2}$ feet long.

How many inches is that?
How do you know?

> I know there are 12 inches in one foot, so there must be 6 inches in $\frac{1}{2}$ foot.

Step Up The lengths of 20 young alligators are shown below. Use this data to complete the line plot on page 211.

$23\frac{1}{2}$ inches	26 inches	27 inches	$23\frac{1}{2}$ inches	26 inches
22 inches	$25\frac{1}{2}$ inches	$27\frac{1}{2}$ inches	25 inches	2 feet
23 inches	26 inches	23 inches	26 inches	$23\frac{1}{2}$ inches
26 inches	$25\frac{1}{2}$ inches	$25\frac{1}{2}$ inches	2 feet	25 inches

I. Draw ● on the line plot to show each length at the bottom of page 210.

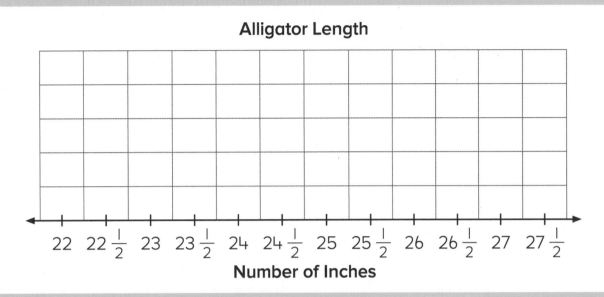

Alligator Length

22   22½   23   23½   24   24½   25   25½   26   26½   27   27½

Number of Inches

2. Use the line plot above to answer these questions.

    a. What is the most common length of alligator? _____

    b. How many alligators are shorter than 26 inches? _____

    c. How many alligators are longer than 2 feet? _____

    d. What is the difference in length between the shortest and longest alligators? _____ inches

    e. If all the alligators grew by ½ inch, how many of them would be 2 feet long? _____

Step Ahead   Write the length of these Australian crocodiles in inches.

Cookie	Bosco	Cassius	Maniac
$9\frac{1}{2}$ feet	$12\frac{1}{2}$ feet	18 feet	$15\frac{2}{3}$ feet
_____ inches	_____ inches	_____ inches	_____ inches

Computation Practice

★ For each division fact, write the multiplication fact you would use to help figure out the quotient. Then write the quotients. Use the classroom clock to time yourself.

Time Taken:

start

$35 \div 5 = \boxed{}$

$\boxed{} \times \boxed{} = \boxed{}$

$36 \div 9 = \boxed{}$

$\boxed{} \times \boxed{} = \boxed{}$

$15 \div 5 = \boxed{}$

$\boxed{} \times \boxed{} = \boxed{}$

$40 \div 8 = \boxed{}$

$\boxed{} \times \boxed{} = \boxed{}$

$32 \div 4 = \boxed{}$

$\boxed{} \times \boxed{} = \boxed{}$

$45 \div 5 = \boxed{}$

$\boxed{} \times \boxed{} = \boxed{}$

$24 \div 6 = \boxed{}$

$\boxed{} \times \boxed{} = \boxed{}$

$36 \div 4 = \boxed{}$

$\boxed{} \times \boxed{} = \boxed{}$

$30 \div 6 = \boxed{}$

$\boxed{} \times \boxed{} = \boxed{}$

$16 \div 4 = \boxed{}$

$\boxed{} \times \boxed{} = \boxed{}$

$28 \div 4 = \boxed{}$

$\boxed{} \times \boxed{} = \boxed{}$

$35 \div 7 = \boxed{}$

$\boxed{} \times \boxed{} = \boxed{}$

$30 \div 5 = \boxed{}$

$\boxed{} \times \boxed{} = \boxed{}$

$28 \div 7 = \boxed{}$

$\boxed{} \times \boxed{} = \boxed{}$

finish

$15 \div 3 = \boxed{}$

$\boxed{} \times \boxed{} = \boxed{}$

$24 \div 4 = \boxed{}$

$\boxed{} \times \boxed{} = \boxed{}$

$20 \div 5 = \boxed{}$

$\boxed{} \times \boxed{} = \boxed{}$

1. Write each number in expanded form.

a.

407,123

_____

_____

b.

398,021

_____

_____

FROM 4.1.5

2. Write a multiplication equation to show each part.
Then write the total of the four partial products.

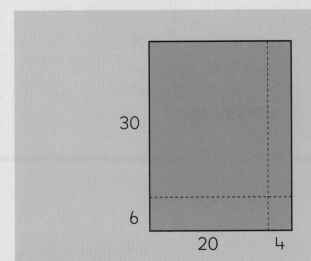

| 36 × 24 |

_____ × _____ = _____

_____ × _____ = _____

_____ × _____ = _____

_____ × _____ = _____

Total _____

FROM 4.6.4

Solve each problem. Show your thinking.

a. Five friends equally share the cost of a gift. The gift costs $60. How much does each person pay?

$_____

b. 54 new books are equally shared among 3 classes. How many new books does each class receive?

_____ books

© ORIGO Education

Step In

Two friends compare their running jumps.
Deana jumped 2 yards. Marcos jumped 5 feet.

What is the difference in length between
their jumps? How do you know?

There are 3 feet
in one yard.

Complete this table.

Yards	1	2	3	5	15	20	35
Feet	3						

How did you calculate the number of feet in 15, 20, and 35 yards?

What does this diagram show?

How many inches are in one yard?

How many inches in 2 yards?
How do you know?

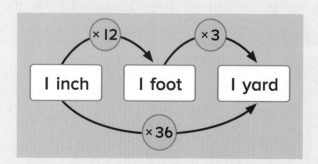

Step Up

1. Convert yards to feet. Show your thinking below.

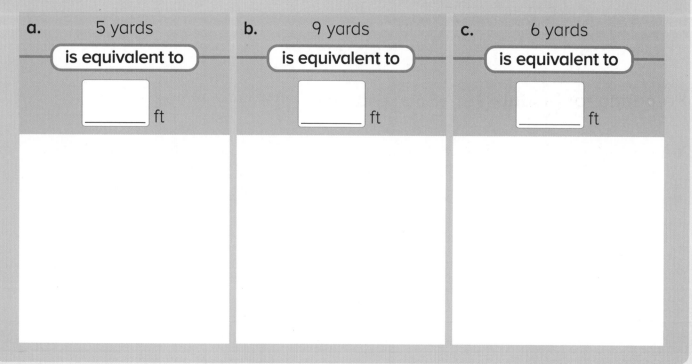

a.   5 yards

is equivalent to

☐ _____ ft

b.   9 yards

is equivalent to

☐ _____ ft

c.   6 yards

is equivalent to

☐ _____ ft

2. Convert yards to feet, and then inches. Show your thinking.

a. 4 yards

is equivalent to

[_____] feet

is equivalent to

[_____] inches

b. 7 yards

is equivalent to

[_____] feet

is equivalent to

[_____] inches

3. Solve each problem. Show your thinking.

a. Hailey's golf ball is 3 yards from the hole. Katherine's ball lands 10 feet from the hole. Whose ball is closer to the hole?

[_____]

b. Andre kicked a ball 42 feet. His dad kicked the ball 3 yards farther. How many feet did his dad kick the ball?

[_____] ft

Step Ahead   Calculate the length of each jump.

Sara jumped 2 yards. Samuel jumped one foot farther than Sara. Cooper jumped one yard less than Samuel. How far did each person jump?

Sara [_____] ft   Samuel [_____] ft   Cooper [_____] ft

Step In

Kimie rides her bike one mile to school each day. James walks 1,200 yards.

Who lives closer to the school?
How do you know?

There are 1,760 yards in one mile.

How could you calculate the number of yards in 5 miles?
What equation could you write?

Gemma wrote these equations.

What steps did she follow? What is the total?

$5 \times 1,000 = 5,000$
$5 \times 700 = 3,500$
$5 \times 60 = 300$
$5 \times 0 = 0$

How could she calculate the number of yards in 7 miles?

Total _____

What does this diagram show?

How could you calculate the number of feet in one mile?

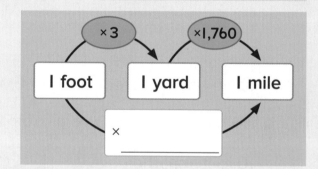

Step Up   1. Circle the distance that makes sense.

a.	the distance around a sporting field		
580 inches	580 feet	580 yards	580 miles

b.	the distance of a plane flight		
465 inches	465 feet	465 yards	465 miles

c.	the length of a baseball bat		
32 inches	32 feet	32 yards	32 miles

d.	the width of a basketball court		
50 inches	50 feet	50 yards	50 miles

2. Convert miles to yards. Remember there are 1,760 yards in one mile.

a.	3 miles		b.	7 miles

a. 3 miles

_____ × _____ = _____

_____ × _____ = _____

_____ × _____ = _____

_____ × _____ = _____

[_____] yards

b. 7 miles

_____ × _____ = _____

_____ × _____ = _____

_____ × _____ = _____

_____ × _____ = _____

[_____] yards

3. Use your answers from Question 2 to calculate the number of feet in each distance. Remember there are 3 feet in one yard.

a. 3 miles

[_____] feet

b. 7 miles

[_____] feet

Step Ahead   Ricardo walked over 7,000 yards as he played 18 holes of golf.

About how many miles did he walk?

[_____] miles

Working Space

Think and Solve

Caleb is 4 times Jessica's age.

Jessica is twice Noah's age.

Noah is one year older than Mary.

Mary is 3 years old.

How old is Caleb? _____ years old

Words at Work Write about the different ways you could convert one mile into different units of length.

_____

_____

_____

_____

_____

_____

_____

_____

_____

_____

_____

_____

_____

I. Round each population to the nearest **ten, hundred,** and **thousand**.

	Population			
	615,959	821,089	529,356	724,612
Nearest ten				
Nearest hundred				
Nearest thousand				

FROM 4.3.3

2. There are 12 inches in one foot and 3 feet in one yard. Complete these to convert yards to feet, or yards to feet and inches.

FROM 4.6.7

a. 2 yards
(is equivalent to)
_____ ft

b. 9 yards
(is equivalent to)
_____ ft

c. 3 yards
(is equivalent to)
_____ ft

d. 4 yards
(is equivalent to)
_____ ft
(is equivalent to)
_____ in

e. 8 yards
(is equivalent to)
_____ ft
(is equivalent to)
_____ in

f. 7 yards
(is equivalent to)
_____ ft
(is equivalent to)
_____ in

The distance from 0 to 1 is one whole. Write the fraction that should be in each box.

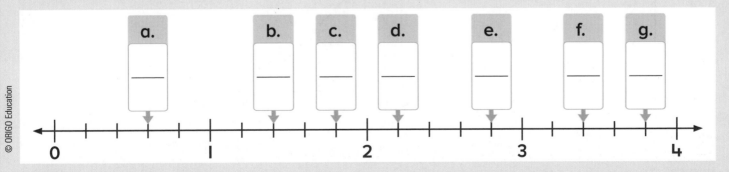

Step In   A quarter-turn tester is a tool that measures a quarter of a full turn.

Other angle testers can be used
to measure other fractions of a full turn.

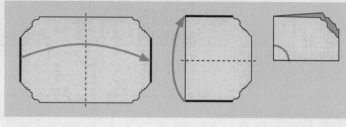

Cut out and fold the angle testers
from the support page.

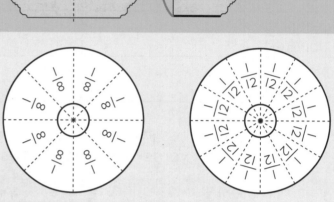

Into how many equal parts has each tester been divided?

When both testers are folded, how many eighths are equivalent to a quarter turn?
How many twelfths are equivalent to a quarter turn?

Step Up   1. Use the eighth-turn tester to measure each angle inside the
shapes below and those on page 221. Write the measurement
beside each arc. Leave the angles blank if they cannot be
measured using this tester.

a.

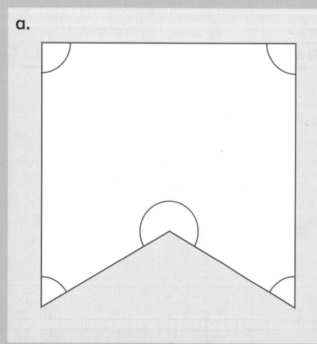

b.

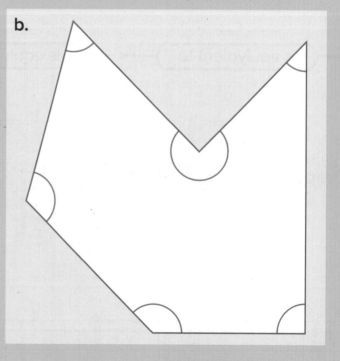

c.

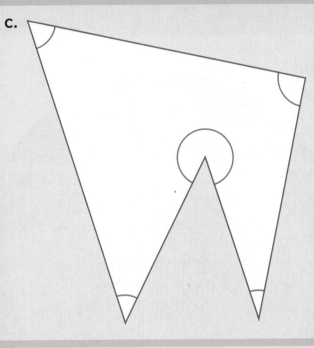

d.

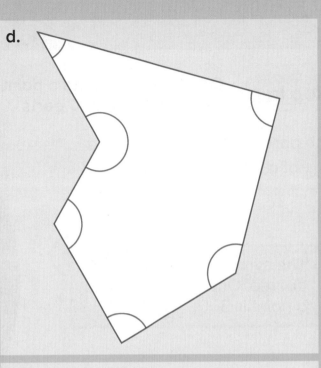

e.

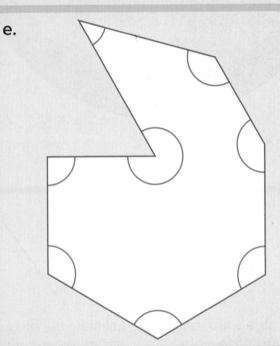

f.

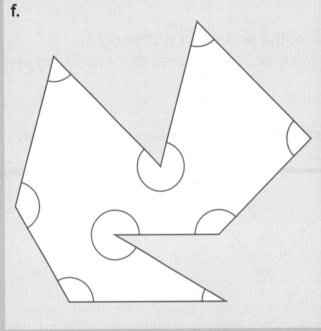

2. Use the twelfth-turn tester to measure each angle inside the shapes shown in Question 1. Write the measurement beside each arc. Some angles will already have a measurement marked, so write beside them.

Step Ahead Use a tester to draw these shapes.

a. A hexagon that has an eight-twelfths angle.

b. A pentagon that has a seven-twelfths angle.

Step In

One full turn around a point can be divided into 360 parts.

Each part is called a **degree** and is $\frac{1}{360}$ of a full turn.

The symbol ° is used for degree. One full turn around a point is 360°.

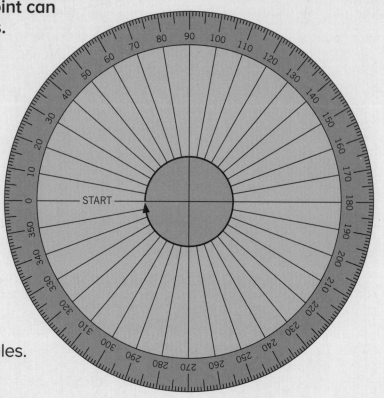

Look at the protractor on the right.
A protractor is a tool used to measure angles.

Follow these steps to use your protractor.

1

Identify the angle arms and rotation point.

2
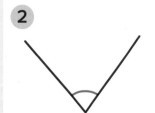
Choose which angle to measure. There are two possible choices.

3
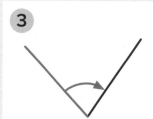
Visualize which angle arm has to move clockwise to the other to show the amount of turn.

4
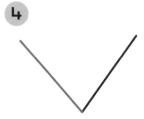
Estimate the amount of turn, for example, is it more or less than 90 degrees?

5

Place the center of the protractor on the rotation point of the angle.

6

Place the protractor's START line on the angle arm that you imagine moving to the other.

7
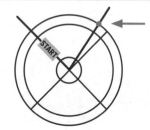
Find the protractor mark that lies on top of the second angle arm.

Use a protractor to measure and label the inside angles of each shape.

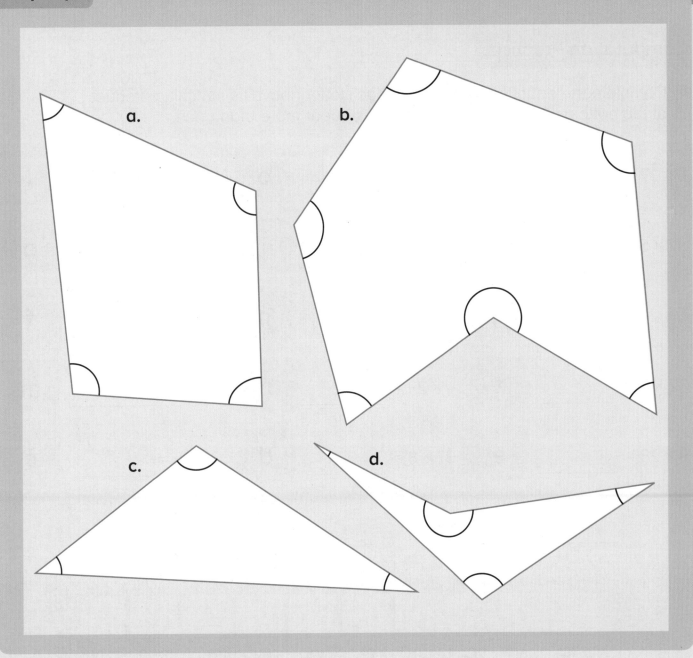

a.

b.

c.

d.

Step Ahead

a. Draw two connecting line segments that show an angle of 60° between them.

b. What fraction of a full turn is 60°?

Computation Practice

★ Complete the equations. Then write each letter above its matching product at the bottom of the page. Some letters appear more than once.

$6 \times 32 =$ ___ **r** $8 \times 45 =$ ___ **o** $9 \times 48 =$ ___ **l**

$17 \times 5 =$ ___ **u** $26 \times 4 =$ ___ **i** $33 \times 9 =$ ___ **a**

$5 \times 23 =$ ___ **q** $37 \times 7 =$ ___ **p** $44 \times 9 =$ ___ **f**

$32 \times 5 =$ ___ **t** $4 \times 29 =$ ___ **n** $7 \times 42 =$ ___ **m**

$9 \times 28 =$ ___ **e** $37 \times 8 =$ ___ **d** $27 \times 4 =$ ___ **c**

$34 \times 6 =$ ___ **s** $53 \times 6 =$ ___ **h**

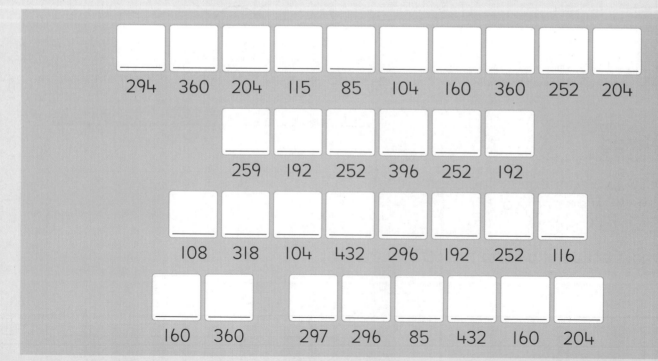

294   360   204   115   85   104   160   360   252   204

259   192   252   396   252   192

108   318   104   432   296   192   252   116

160   360   297   296   85   432   160   204

Ongoing Practice

1. Draw ● to show these students' scores on the line plot.

18	15	12	19	19	17
20	11	13	19	20	16
15	17	18	20	16	15

Math Test Scores

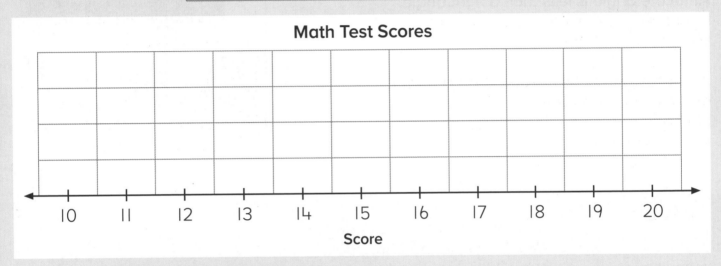

Score

2. Circle the distance that makes sense.

a. the school record for throwing a discus			
23 inches	23 feet	23 yards	23 miles

b. the distance of a long bus trip			
825 inches	825 feet	825 yards	825 miles

Preparing for Module 7

Each large shape is one whole. Complete each equation to show how much is shaded. Write the total as a common fraction then as a mixed number.

a.

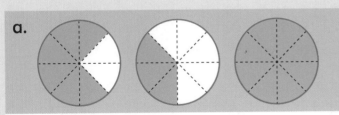

—— + —— + —— = —— =

b.

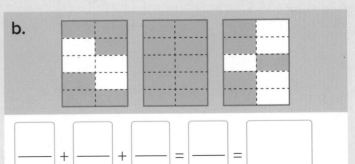

—— + —— + —— = —— =

Step In

A right angle is one-fourth of a full turn.

How many degrees does that equal? How do you know?
Find two right angles in the picture.
Mark them with a blue arc.

An acute angle is less than a right angle.
Find two acute angles in the picture.
Mark them with a red arc.

An obtuse angle is greater than a right angle, but less than a half turn.
Find two obtuse angles in the picture.
Mark them with a green arc.

Step Up

1. Use a protractor to help you find these angles.
   - Write A next to the acute angles.
   - Write R next to the right angles.
   - Write O next to the obtuse angles.

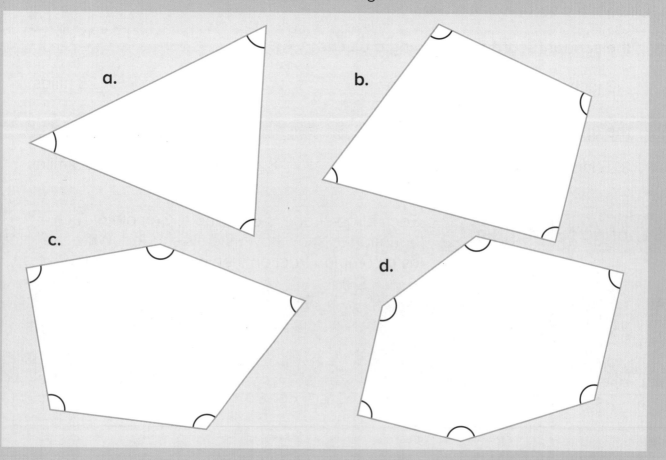

a.

b.

c.

d.

2. Triangles can be named acute, right, or obtuse based on the size of their greatest angle. In each triangle below, circle the greatest angle.

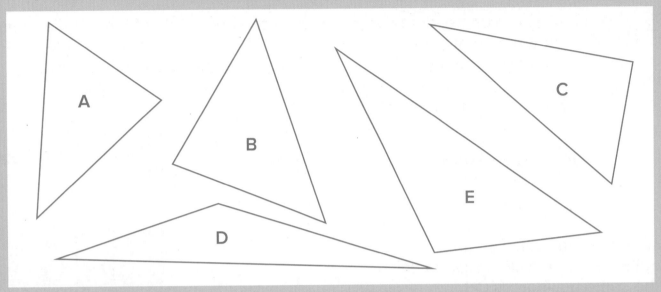

3. Use a protractor to measure each angle you circled in Question 2. Write the values below.

A ___ °	B ___ °	C ___ °	D ___ °	E ___ °

4. Use your measurements from Question 3 to answer these questions about the triangles in Question 2.

a. Which triangles are acute triangles? _____

b. Which triangles are right triangles? _____

c. Which triangles are obtuse triangles? _____

Step Ahead	For each of these, draw a triangle that shows the angle. Mark the angle with an arc.

a. one obtuse angle	b. one right angle

Step In

Angles can be identified by labeling the endpoints of their angle arms and the point where the arms meet. When using points to name an angle, the point that refers to the vertex must be in the middle.

This angle can be called Angle ROS.

What other name could be used?
How do you know?

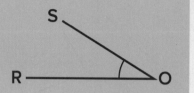

RO is one of the angle arms. What is the other angle arm?

Look at this diagram.
Imagine OA turned clockwise to finish at the same position as OB.

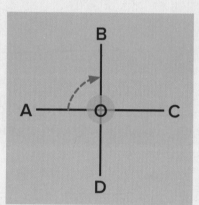

What fraction of a full turn would OA have made?

How many degrees would it have turned? How do you know?

What does that tell you about Angle AOB?

> I think it is one-fourth of a full turn. A full turn is 360 degrees, so I need to figure out one-fourth of 360.

Step Up

1. Use the clues to calculate the size of each angle in the diagram. Do not use a protractor. Show your thinking.

Clues

- Angle **BOD** is 40°.
- Angle **COD** is half of Angle **BOD**.
- Angle **AOB** is the same size as Angle **BOD**.

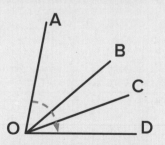

a.
Angle **COD** is _____ °

b.
Angle **AOB** is _____ °

c.
Angle **AOD** is _____ °

d.
Angle **AOC** is _____ °

2. Look at the diagram. Use the clues to calculate the size of each angle.
Do not use a protractor. Show your thinking.

Clues	
• Angle **AOB** is 30°.	• Angle **DOE** is 30°.
• Angle **BOC** is 30°.	• Angle **EOF** is 30°.
• Angle **COD** is 30°.	• Angle **FOG** is 30°.

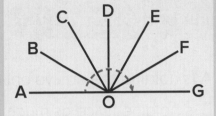

a.
Angle **AOC** is _____ °

b.
Angle **AOD** is _____ °

c.
Angle **EOG** is _____ °

d.
Angle **AOE** is _____ °

e.
Angle **BOE** is _____ °

f.
Angle **AOG** is _____ °

3. Look at the diagram in Question 2. Name three angles that are **less than 90°**.

_____ _____ _____

4. Look at the diagram in Question 2. Name three angles that are **greater than 90°**.

_____ _____ _____

Step Ahead   Look at the diagram in Question 2 above. Write these angle sizes.

Angle **BOD** is _____ °

Half of Angle **BOD** is _____ °

Angle **BOF** is _____ °

Half of Angle **BOF** is _____ °

Angle **BOC** is _____ °

One-third of Angle **BOC** is _____ °

Angle **DOG** is _____ °

One-third of Angle **DOG** is _____ °

Think and Solve

A is holding the equivalent amount as B.

B is holding twice as much as C.

C is holding 10 L.

A, B, and C are holding a total of [   ] L

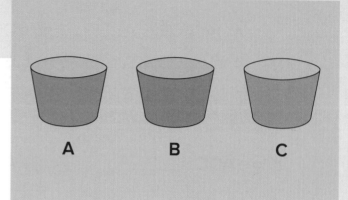

A   B   C

Words at Work

Write the answer for each clue in the grid. Use words from the list. Some words are not used.

Clues Across

1. There are three feet in one ___.

3. There are 1,760 yards in one ___.

7. One foot is the eqivalent ___ as 12 inches.

8. There are 360 degrees in ___ full turn around a point.

9. An ___ angle is greater than a right angle but less than a half turn.

Clues Down

2. An acute ___ is less than a right angle.

4. A yard is equivalent to 36 ___.

5. A ___ angle is one-fourth of a full turn.

6. A protractor is a ___ used to measure angles.

right
length
angle
inches
obtuse
half
full
tool
one
yard
acute
mile
feet

Ongoing Practice

1. These line plots show the distances run by an athlete during training.

FROM 3.6.12

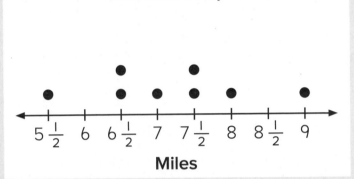

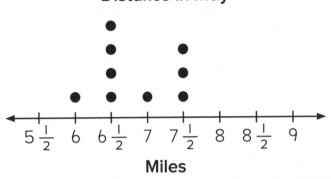

a. In which month did the athlete train for the greater number of days?

b. In which month did the athlete run the greater total distance?

c. What is the difference between the total distances run in April and May? _____ miles

2. Use a protractor to measure and label the inside angles of the shape.

FROM 4.6.10

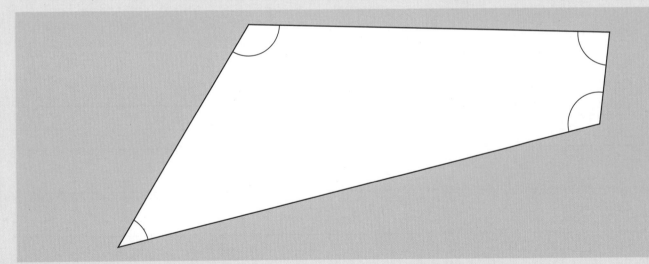

Preparing for Module 7

Write each whole number as a fraction. Use what you know about multiples to help you.

$1 = \dfrac{\quad}{2}$ $2 = \dfrac{\quad}{2}$ $3 = \dfrac{\quad}{2}$ $4 = \dfrac{\quad}{2}$ $5 = \dfrac{\quad}{2}$

6 Mathematical modeling task

Players of an online game earn 85 bronze coins when they win a tournament. They also earn 265 silver coins every time they share resources with another player and 1,155 gold coins when they pass a level. When players start the game, they are given 150 silver coins for free.

Cooper starts the game on Saturday morning. By the end of the day, he has passed five levels, won seven tournaments, and shared resources with three other players.

a. How many of each type of coin does Cooper have at the end of Saturday?

b. Bronze coins are worth 3 points, silver coins 5 points, and gold coins 9 points. How many points does Cooper have in total at the end of Saturday? Show your thinking.

 Share why your chose this strategy.

Estimate the size of each of these angles: AOB, BOC, BOD.
Do not use a protractor. Show your thinking.

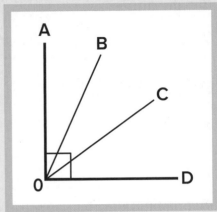

AOB is equivalent to _____ .

I think this because ...

_____

_____

BOC is equivalent to _____ .

I think this because ...

_____

_____

BOD is equivalent to _____ .

I think this because ...

_____

_____

Share your estimates with another student. They can write their feedback below.

I agree/disagree with your estimates because ...

Feedback from:

Discuss how the feedback helped to challenge or confirm your original estimates.

STUDENT GLOSSARY

Acute angle

Any angle less than 90 degrees (90°).

Angle arm

Each of the two rays that join at a vertex to form an angle.

Arc

A symbol used to show the angle created by two rays that join at a vertex.

Commutative property of multiplication

This property means that two numbers can be multiplied in any order and the product will not change. For example, 3 × 5 = 15 and 5 × 3 = 15. These facts are commonly called turnaround facts.

Composite number

A whole number that has more than two whole number factors.

Convert

To write a value as an equivalent value. For example, in measurement, to rewrite 12 inches as one foot, or 1,000 meters as one kilometer.

Decimeter (dm)

A metric unit of length. One decimeter is equivalent to 10 centimeters and 10 decimeters is equivalent to one meter. One decameter is a little shorter than 4 inches.

Degree (°)

One unit of angle measure. There are 360 degrees in a full turn or a full rotation around a point.

Dekameter (dam)

A metric unit of length (distance). One decameter is equivalent to 10 meters and 10 decameters is equivalent to one hectometer. One decameter is a little shorter than 11 yards.

STUDENT GLOSSARY

Distributive property of multiplication

This property means that one or both factors can be split into place-value parts, then each part can be multiplied separately. The partial products are then added to find the final product. For example, 23 × 34 = 20 × 30 + 20 × 4 + 3 × 30 + 3 × 4 = 600 + 80 + 90 + 12 = 782. The partial-products strategy uses this property.

End points

The non-joining ends of the two angle arms (rays) that meet to form an angle. For example, in this angle (SOR), the endpoints of the angle arms are labeled S and R.

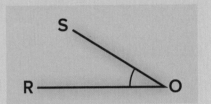

Factor

A whole number that evenly divides another whole number. For example, 4 and 5 are both factors of 20.

Full turn

A full rotation of 360 degrees around a point.

Hectometer (hm)

A metric unit of length (distance). One kilometer is equivalent to 10 hectometers. One hectometer is a little shorter than 110 yards.

Hundred thousands

In the base-ten number system, this is the first place to the left of the ten-thousands place. The value of any digit in this place is described as a number of groups of one hundred thousand. For example, in 642,807, the value of the 6 is 6 groups of one hundred thousand.

Thousands			Ones		
H	T	O	H	T	O
6	4	2	8	0	7

STUDENT GLOSSARY

Kilometer (km)

A metric unit of length (distance). One kilometer is equivalent to 1,000 meters and is about $\frac{6}{10}$ of a mile.

Mile (mi)

A unit of length (distance). One mile is equivalent to 1,760 yards.

Milliliter (mL)

A metric unit of capacity. 1,000 milliliters is equivalent to one liter. One teaspoon holds about 5 milliliters.

Millimeter (mm)

A metric unit of length. 1,000 milliliters is equivalent to one meter. One inch is about 25 millimeters.

Millions

In the base-ten number system, it is the first place to the left of the hundred thousands place. The value of any digit in the millions place of a number is described as a number of groups of one million. For example, in 5,642,807, the value of the 5 is 5 groups of one million.

Millions			Thousands			Ones		
H	T	O	H	T	O	H	T	O
		5	6	4	2	8	0	7

Mixed number

A whole number and a common fraction added together, and written without the addition symbol. For example, $2 + \frac{1}{2} = 2\frac{1}{2}$.

Multiple

The product of a number multiplied by another whole number. For example, the multiples of 4 include 4, 8, 12, and 16.

STUDENT GLOSSARY

Obtuse angle

Any angle greater than 90 degrees (90°) but less than 180 degrees (180°).

Prime number

Any whole number greater than zero that has exactly two unique factors — itself and one.

Protractor

A tool used to measure angles.

Relationship

Describes how two or more sets of numbers, values, or objects relate to each other. For example, if Bag A weighs 45 kg and Bag B weighs 15 kg, then the relationship can be described as Bag A is equivalent to Bag B × 3, or Bag A is three times as heavy as Bag B.

Right angle

Any angle equal to 90 degrees (90°).

Rotation point

The vertex of an angle.

Square centimeter (cm²)

A unit of area that describes a square with sides that are one centimeter long.

Square yard (yd²)

A unit of area that describes a square with sides that are one yard long.

STUDENT GLOSSARY

Times as long

A phrase used to describe the relationship between two lengths, where one length is a multiple of the other length. For example, 12 inches is three times as long as 4 inches.

Times as many

A phrase used to describe the relationship between two numbers or quantities, where one number or quantity is a multiple of the other. For example, 100,000 is 10 times as many as 10,000.

Working Space